Key Stage 3
Developing Numeracy

CALCULATIONS

ACTIVITIES FOR TEACHING NUMERACY

year
7

Hilary Koll and Steve Mills

A & C BLACK

Contents

Written methods

Calculator methods

Checking results

Answers

Published 2003 by A & C Black Publishers Limited
37 Soho Square, London W1D 3QZ
www.acblack.com

ISBN 0-7136-6468-1

Copyright text © Hilary Koll and Steve Mills, 2003
Copyright illustrations © David Benham, 2003
Copyright cover illustration © Paul Cemmick, 2003
Editors: Lynne Williamson and Marie Lister
Designer: Kim Sillitoe

The authors and publishers would like to thank David Chadwick, Corinne McCrum and Jane McNeill for their advice in producing this series of books.

A CIP catalogue record for this book is available from the British Library.

Printed in Great Britain by St Edmundsbury Press Ltd, Bury St Edmunds, Suffolk.

A & C Black uses paper produced with elemental chlorine-free pulp, harvested from managed sustainable forests.

Introduction

Key Stage 3 **Developing Numeracy: Calculations** is a series of photocopiable resources for Years 7, 8 and 9, designed to be used during maths lessons. The books focus on the Calculations strand of the Key Stage 3 National Strategy *Framework for teaching mathematics*.

Each book supports the teaching of mathematics by providing a series of activities that develop essential skills in numeracy. The activities aim to reinforce learning and develop the skills and understanding explored during whole-class teaching. Each task provides practice and consolidation of an objective contained in the framework document. On the whole the activities are designed for pupils to work on independently, either individually or in pairs, although occasionally some pupils may need support.

The activities in **Calculations Year 7** relate to the following topics:

- number operations and the relationships between them;
- mental methods and rapid recall of number facts;
- written methods;
- calculator methods;
- checking results.

How to use this book

Each double-page spread is based around a Year 7 objective. The spread has three main sections labelled A, B and C, and ends with a challenge (**Now try this!**). The work grows increasingly difficult from A through to C, and the 'Now try this!' challenge reinforces and extends pupils' learning. The activities provide the teacher with an opportunity to make informal assessments: for example, checking that pupils are developing mental strategies, have grasped the main teaching points, or whether they have any misunderstandings.

This double-page structure can be used in a variety of ways: for example, following whole-class teaching the pupils can begin to work through both sheets and will experience gradually more complex questions, or the teacher can choose the most appropriate starting points for each group in the class, with some pupils starting at A and others at B or C. This allows differentiation for mixed-ability groups. 'Now try this!' provides a greater challenge for more able pupils. It can involve 'Using and Applying' concepts and skills, and provides an opportunity for classroom discussion. Where appropriate, pupils can be asked to finish tasks for homework.

The instructions are presented clearly to enable pupils to work independently. There are also opportunities for pupils to work in pairs and groups, to encourage discussion and co-operation. A calculator icon indicates whether or not calculators should be used for different parts of the activities. Where there is no icon, the teacher or pupils may choose whether or not to use them. Brief notes are provided at the foot of each page to assist the pupil or classroom assistant, or parent if the sheets are used for homework. Remind the pupils to read these before beginning the activity.

In some cases, the pupils will need to record their workings on a separate piece of paper, and it is suggested that these workings are handed in with the activity sheets. The pupils will also need to record their answers to some of the 'Now try this!' challenges on another piece of paper.

Organisation

Very little equipment is needed, other than the essential rulers, pencils and so on, but for some activity sheets pupils will need algebraic calculators. These activity sheets allow opportunities for pupils to explore keys and interpret the display on the calculator, considering issues such as rounding. It is important in some cases that the calculators used have certain keys, for example a sign change key. During the teaching input, discuss how such keys can be shown in different ways on different calculators, for example $+/-$ or $(-)$.

To help teachers select appropriate learning experiences for pupils, the activities are grouped into sections within the book to match the objectives in the Key Stage 3 National Strategy *Yearly teaching programmes*. However, the activities do not have to be used in the order given. The sheets are intended to support, rather than direct, the teacher's planning.

Some activities can be made easier or more challenging by masking or substituting some of the numbers. You may wish to re-use some pages by copying them onto card and laminating them, or by enlarging them onto A3 paper. They could also be made into OHTs for whole-class use.

Teachers' notes

Further brief notes, containing specific instructions or points to be raised during the first part of the lesson, are provided for particular sheets (see pages 6–7).

Whole-class oral and mental starters

The following activities provide some practical ideas to support the main teaching part of the lesson, and can be carried out before pupils use the activity sheets.

Mental methods and rapid recall of number facts

Number strip

Write a number fact on a strip of card or thick paper (for example, $3567 + 1231 = 4798$; $16 \times 12 = 192$; or $285 \div 15 = 19$). Wrap a narrow piece of paper around the strip of card, so that it can slide sideways to mask one of the numbers or the operator sign. Hold up the strip and ask pupils to find the hidden number or sign. You could build up a collection of number strips to use throughout the year.

Complements

Call out positive whole numbers and ask pupils to give the complements to 100: for example, if you call out 73, the pupils should respond with 27, as $73 + 27 = 100$. Similarly, decimals (with one or two decimal places) can be called out and pupils asked to give complements to 1: for example, 0.8 and 0.2, or 0.54 and 0.46.

Speed limits

Write the number 30, 40, 60 or 70 in a circle on the board. Explain that this is the 'speed limit'. Ask calculation questions and have pupils say whether the answer is greater than the speed limit ('Speeding'), exactly on the speed limit ('OK') or under the speed limit ('Slow'). Questions could include multiplication and division facts, doubles and halves, and addition and subtraction questions. For example, *I'm travelling at a speed which is 6 times faster than 8 miles per hour, … half as fast as 76 mph, … 17 miles per hour slower than 61 mph.*

Rapid recall

Give each pupil two sets of 0–9 digit cards. Play 'show me' activities: for example: *Show me double 37; Show me the product of 7 and 9; Show me the value of 8 squared.* Pupils 'show' a number by holding one or two digit cards in the air.

Written methods

Write it

Split the class into two teams and give each team a digit card, for example 4 and 7. Write a question (using any operation) on the board, to be solved using a column method. Explain that the teams will score a point each time their digit appears in the written method. Invite a pupil to complete the method on the board and award the points. The teams can choose their own digit once a question is written, if preferred.

Calculator methods

Percentages

Split the class into up to five teams. Write five percentages across the board in increasing size, for example 12%, 17%, 29%, 48%, 73%. Beneath each percentage write a number decreasing in size, for example 180, 120, 90, 88, 50. Use these as five different percentage questions (12% of 180, 17% of 120, and so on). Ask each team to choose one question that they think has the highest value. They should then find the values of all five percentages. The team (or teams) with the highest value scores a point.

Teachers' notes

Number operations and the relationships between them

Pages 8 & 9

Explain that for parts A and C it is not necessary to find the answers, but only to suggest an appropriate method that does not use multiplication or division. These activities will help you assess the pupils' understanding of these operations.

Pages 10 & 11

When the pupils are tackling the 'Now try this!' challenge, encourage them to think of negative integers and fractions or decimals as well as positive whole numbers when deciding on the truth of the statements. Discuss that, for a statement to be true, it must be true for all cases, but that a statement can be proved false by providing just one example that does not work. Go through the answers carefully.

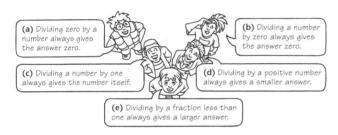

(a) Dividing zero by a number always gives the answer zero.

(b) Dividing a number by zero always gives the answer zero.

(c) Dividing a number by one always gives the number itself.

(d) Dividing by a positive number always gives a smaller answer.

(e) Dividing by a fraction less than one always gives a larger answer.

Pages 12 & 13

During the first part of the lesson, remind the pupils of the order of precedence of operations, for example by discussing BODMAS or BIDMAS. Some teachers prefer to introduce pupils to the term BIDMAS rather than BODMAS, where the 'I' stands for 'indices'. Discuss this with the class and explain that either word can remind them of the order of precedence of operations.

In part C, pupils could be reminded that the formula of a triangle applies to non right-angled triangles too, as h stands for the height perpendicular to the base.

Pages 14 & 15

It is important pupils understand that an inverse operation can undo a previous operation: for example, subtracting 36 can be undone by adding 36. Revise that the inverse of addition is subtraction, the inverse of multiplication is division, and vice versa. Remind pupils that when a number of operations take place, the order of the inverse operations should be reversed.

Pages 16 & 17

Some teachers prefer to introduce pupils to the term BIDMAS rather than BODMAS, where the 'I' stands for 'indices'. Discuss this with the class and explain that either word can remind them of the order of precedence of operations.

Pages 18 & 19

Pupils in Year 7 are expected to know multiplication facts up to 12×12. Begin the first part of the lesson by encouraging quick recall of these facts. For the activities in part C, encourage pupils to make 'mental jottings'. Pupils can be asked to a check the ISBN numbers of other books in the same way.

Mental methods and rapid recall of number facts

Pages 20 & 21

Revise the notation for squaring a number and finding a square root, e.g. 5^2 and $\sqrt{25}$. Explore the relationship between a square number and its root, encouraging pupils to describe these relationships in words: for example, *nine squared equals 81 and the square root of 81 is nine.* Explain to pupils that once a number fact is known then other related facts are also known: for example, 90 squared is 8100, so the square root of 8100 is 90.

Pages 22 & 23

Remind pupils of strategies for multiplying and dividing by 10, 100 and 1000, ensuring that they do not just 'add or subtract zeros'. (The idea of adding or subtracting zeros does not work for decimals: 0.36×10 does not equal 0.360.) Discuss strategies which involve moving the digits across the columns, with the decimal point 'staying where it is'. Some pupils may benefit from seeing this practically, for example by moving digit cards.

Pages 24 & 25

Pupils in Year 7 are expected to know the doubles of all two-digit numbers and their corresponding halves; and the related doubles of multiples of 10, 100 and 1000: for example, double 73, double 730, double 7300. They are also expected to know related decimal facts, e.g. double 7.3 and double 0.73. Revise these at the start of the lesson, ensuring that you use a range of vocabulary: *twice, half, multiplied by two, divided by two, plus,* and so on.

For pupils who do not know these facts by heart, demonstrate a suitable strategy, e.g. splitting a number into parts (partitioning) and doubling each part separately before adding the answers. Encourage pupils to find their own strategies for finding answers to doubling and halving questions.

Pages 26 & 27

When teaching new mental methods it is often a good idea to show the strategy visually, as is done here. Encourage pupils to appreciate that it is sometimes easier to add multiples of 10 or 100, or (in part C) whole numbers, and then to adjust the answer. Provide several examples of each of these types on the board before pupils begin the activities.

Pages 28 & 29

Revise partitioning before pupils begin these activities. Explain that this is not always the most effective method: for example, 78 + 99 might be done more easily by adding 100 and subtracting 1. For pupils tackling part C, remind them that when finding the difference between two numbers that are either side of a multiple of 10, 100 or 1000, it is easier to use that multiple as a 'stepping stone'. For example, 8003 − 7998 is most easily done by counting up from the smaller number to 8000 and then counting on up to 8003.

Pages 30 & 31

Remind pupils that a factor is a number that divides exactly into another. Factors often come in pairs: for example, 3 and 4 are factors of 12 and $3 \times 4 = 12$. Explain that you can sometimes use factors to reach answers to calculations more quickly. For example, 5.4×30 can be thought of as $5.4 \times 10 \times 3$, so $5.4 \times 30 = 54 \times 3 = 162$.

Pages 34 & 35

Encourage pupils to discuss the methods they use for finding percentages of numbers mentally. Stress that all strategies are valid if they always give the correct answer and that different questions may require different strategies.

Written methods

Pages 38 & 39

Begin the lesson by discussing the meaning of the term 'column method' and examining different methods that can be used to perform written addition and subtraction of three- and four-digit numbers. Explain that, for these pages, all calculations should be done using column methods.

Pages 40 & 41

Revise that when adding and subtracting decimals it is possible to treat them in exactly the same way as whole numbers. Stress the importance of the digits being lined up in the correct columns and point out that the decimal points should line up also. Watch out for pupils who line the digits up from the right of each number and discuss the value of each digit to correct this error. Encourage pupils to check their answers by approximation to ensure that sensible answers are given.

Pages 46 & 47

If the pupils are confident with a different method of division that consistently provides a correct answer, then they could be encouraged to use it instead of the method shown. Discuss these different methods if appropriate.

Calculator methods

Pages 50 & 51

The pupils will require an algebraic calculator with sign change, brackets, square and square root keys. In part C, remind them to put brackets around both what is on the top and what is on the bottom of the division line if they are doing the calculation in one go.

Pages 52 & 53

In part C, discuss the two main strategies for solving the following question using a calculator:

Sanjay has £477. He buys as many CDs as he can with his money. They cost £13 each. How much money does he have left over?

One method is as follows:

Divide 477 by 13. Subtract the whole number part of the answer (− 36). Now multiply the remaining decimal by the price of the CD (× 13). This will tell you how much Sanjay has left.

A second method is as follows:

Divide 477 by 13. Look at the whole number part (36). Enter this whole number into your calculator and multiply it by the price of the CD (× 13). This will tell you how much Sanjay spent on CDs. Now subtract this amount from Sanjay's money (£477) to see how much he will have left.

Encourage the pupils to use both methods and to say which they prefer.

Pages 54 & 55

The pupils can be introduced to the mnemonic ABC when using a calculator, where A stands for 'approximate', B for 'buttons' (as in using the calculator buttons), and C for 'check'. This can help them to remember the importance of thinking before, during and after using the calculator to ensure they reach a sensible answer.

Checking results

Pages 56 & 57

The different checking strategies should each be taught separately: for example, using odd and even rules, looking at the last digit, doing an approximation. When several strategies have been taught, provide questions and possible answers on the board, and ask pupils to suggest which checking strategies they might choose.

Crucial operations

A

Imagine the ☒ key on your calculator does not work.

1. Write what you would key in to help you answer these questions.

(a)	482 × 2
(b)	167 × 3
(c)	(568 × 10) + 47
(d)	748 × 5
(e)	239 × 11
(f)	431 × 11
(g)	941 × 9
(h)	22 × ? = 1034
(i)	58 × ? = 4176
(j)	? × 72 = 2448
(k)	? × 83 = 1411
(l)	156 × 101
(m)	342 × 99

482 + 482

2390 + 239

You do not have to find the answers. **!**

Remember what happens when you multiply a number by 10. **!**

2. Discuss your methods with a partner.

B

Fill in the missing numbers.

(a) 36 × ☐ = 0   36 × ☐ = 36   36 + ☐ = 36

(b) ☐ × 47 = 47   47 − ☐ = 47   47 × ☐ = 0

(c) 58 ÷ ☐ = 1   58 × ☐ = 0   58 ÷ ☐ = 58

(d) ☐ + 95 = 95   ☐ × 95 = 95   ☐ ÷ 95 = 0

 For part B, remember that any number multiplied by zero is zero, and any number multiplied by one is the same number.

Developing Numeracy
Calculations
Year 7
© A & C BLACK

1. Imagine the $\div$ key on your calculator does not work. Write what you would key in to help you answer these questions.

You do not have to find the answers.

(a) 243 ÷ 81 $243 - 81 - 81 - 81$

(b) 237 ÷ 79

(c) 204 ÷ 68

(d) 292 ÷ ? = 73

(e) 376 ÷ ? = 94

(f) ? ÷ 18 = 43

(g) ? ÷ 29 = 85

(h) ? ÷ 58 = 72

(i) ? ÷ 96 = 129

2. Here are four different ways of calculating £4.99 × 42.

I would add together 42 lots of 4.99.

I would multiply 42 by 5 first and then subtract 42p.

I would write out the calculation like this:
    4.99
 ×   42

I would multiply 42 by 10, halve the answer and then subtract 0.42.

(a) Whose method do you think is easiest? _____

(b) Explain how easy or difficult you think each method would be, and why.

Kim _____

Tom _____

Dev _____

Jo _____

NOW TRY THIS!

- For each of these questions, write four different methods that you could use to solve it. Decide which you think is the most effective method, and why.

   (a) £5.01 × 17   **(b)** £1.99 × 38   **(c)** 49 × £3.15

- Discuss your methods with a partner. Do you agree on which method is best?

In C1, use estimating and rounding to help you work out what you would key in for questions (a) to (e). There are many different ways to do calculations mentally. The best method is the one that helps you to reach the answer most easily and quickly.

Division decisions

A Choose the most appropriate answer for each question.

If there are **two** appropriate answers, choose only one.

(a) 68 people are split into teams of eight. How many teams are there and how many people are left over? _8 r 4_

(b) Mr Collins shares £42.50 equally between the five members of his family. How much does each person get? _____

(c) I have 35 photos. I can fit four on a page in my album. How many pages will have photos on? _____

(d) Three identical sacks of potatoes weigh a total of 25.5 kg. What is the mass in kilograms of each sack of potatoes? _____

(e) A piece of string 68 cm long is cut into eight equal pieces. What is the length in centimetres of each piece? _____

(f) A piece of string 68 cm long is cut into 8-cm long pieces. How many pieces of this length can be cut? _____

(g) 34 children go on a school trip. If four children can fit in a car, how many cars are needed? _____

(h) Lesley has £85 to spend on cinema tickets. She can buy ten, leaving no change. How much are the tickets? _____

(i) Pete arranges 36 coins into four equal piles. How many are in each pile and how many are left over? _____

(j) A doctor has to see 51 patients. If he can see six patients per hour, how many hours will it take him? _____

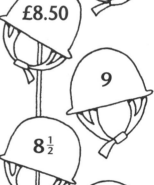

B Follow these instructions five times.

☆ Write a [prime number] between 50 and 100 (for example 79).
☆ Choose a number between 3 and 9 and divide the prime number by this.
☆ Write your answer in three different ways.

(79 ÷ 4) = 19.75 or $19\frac{3}{4}$ or 19 r 3

Remember that a **prime number** is a number with only two factors, itself and 1. The prime numbers between 50 and 100 are 53, 59, 61, 67, 71, 73, 79, 83, 89 and 97.

Division decisions

C

1. Use a calculator to do the divisions. Round the answer shown on the calculator to give a sensible answer. Think carefully about whether to round up or down for each situation.

(a) A machine puts matches into matchboxes. Each box holds 175 matches. How many boxes can be filled with 5937 matches?

Calculator: _33.925714_

Sensible answer: _33_

(b) Mrs Owen earns £148 per week. In how many weeks will she earn enough to buy a car costing £4200?

Calculator: _____

Sensible answer: _____

(c) Dinesh buys four CDs that cost £47.93 in total. What is the average price of each CD?

Calculator: _____

Sensible answer: _____

(d) Li earns £11 an evening for babysitting. About how many evenings must she babysit to earn enough to buy a pair of trainers costing £89?

Calculator: _____

Sensible answer: _____

(e) The total cost of Sam's phone calls is £42.90. He made 36 calls. What is the average cost of each call?

Calculator: _____

Sensible answer: _____

(f) A soap opera lasts for 23 minutes. How many episodes can be recorded back-to-back on a four-hour tape?

Calculator: _____

Sensible answer: _____

(g) A machine takes 45 seconds to fill and seal a tube of sweets. How many tubes can it fill and seal in 13 minutes?

Calculator: _____

Sensible answer: _____

(h) A lorry carries four identical crates weighing a total of 328.75 kg. About how many grams does each crate weigh?

Calculator: _____

Sensible answer: _____

2. Discuss your decisions with a partner.

● Write whether these statements are true or false. Give three examples for each.

(a) Dividing zero by a number always gives the answer zero.

(b) Dividing a number by zero always gives the answer zero.

(c) Dividing a number by one always gives the number itself.

(d) Dividing by a positive number always gives a smaller answer.

(e) Dividing by a fraction less than one always gives a larger answer.

 In part C, think carefully about the situation in each question. Sometimes a number like 5.78 is rounded **down** where 5 is a more sensible answer than 5.8 or 6 (for example, how many people can fit into a car).

Developing Numeracy
Calculations
Year 7
© A & C BLACK

11

The laws of arithmetic

1. Draw arcs to show the easiest order in which to multiply these numbers. Rewrite the sums and find the answers.

(a) $4 \times 7 \times 5$ = $\underline{20 \times 7 = 140}$ **(b)** $2 \times 13 \times 5$ = _____

(c) $8 \times 12 \times 5$ = _____   **(d)** $5 \times 9 \times 4$ = _____

(e) $2 \times 16 \times 5$ = _____   **(f)** $9 \times 4 \times 5$ = _____

(g) $12 \times 3 \times 10$ = _____   **(h)** $14 \times 9 \times 5$ = _____

(i) $27 \times 5 \times 2$ = _____   **(j)** $4 \times 25 \times 15$ = _____

(k) $4 \times 13 \times 2.5$ = _____   **(l)** $18 \times 4 \times 2.5$ = _____

2. Answer these questions. Solve the part in brackets first.

(a) $3 \times (2 \times 5)$ = _____   **(b)** $(3 \times 2) \times 5$ = _____

(c) $(10 \times 4) \times 6$ = _____   **(d)** $10 \times (4 \times 6)$ = _____

(e) $5 \times (3 \times 4)$ = _____   **(f)** $(5 \times 3) \times 4$ = _____

(g) $(9 \times 2) \times 2$ = _____   **(h)** $9 \times (2 \times 2)$ = _____

3. Write a fact about multiplication that you have used to answer A1 or A2.

_____

_____

B These cards can be rearranged to make questions.

$$(\quad) \quad 8 \quad 4 \quad 2 \quad + \quad \times$$

> When using both addition and multiplication, the order is important. Always do the part in brackets first.

Find a question to match each of these answers.

> Use all seven cards in each question, and use each card only once.

$(2 \times 8) + 4$

(a) 20 = _____   **(b)** 16 = _____

(c) 34 = _____   **(d)** 24 = _____

(e) 40 = _____   **(f)** 48 = _____

The **commutative law** of multiplication means that you can multiply numbers in any order and the answer will be the same. The **associative law** says that when you multiply more than two numbers together, you can group them in any way and the answer will be the same.

Developing Numeracy
Calculations
Year 7
© A & C BLACK

The laws of arithmetic

C **1.**

You can use this formula to find the area of a triangle, where b is the base and h is the perpendicular height:

Area = $\frac{1}{2} \times b \times h$

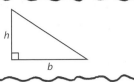

(a) Tick the calculations you could use to find the area of this triangle:

$12 \times 8 \times \frac{1}{2}$ ✓ $8 \times 12 \times \frac{1}{2}$ ☐ $\frac{1}{2} \times 8 \times 12$ ☐

$4 \times 8 \times 12$ ☐ $8 \times 12 \div 2$ ☐ $\frac{1}{2} \times 12 \times 12$ ☐

$12 \div 2 \times 8$ ☐ $12 \times \frac{1}{2} \times 8$ ☐ $\frac{1}{2} \times (12 \times 8)$ ☐

$8 \div 2 \times 12$ ☐ $(\frac{1}{2} \times 12) \times 8$ ☐ $(8 \times \frac{1}{2}) \times 12$ ☐

(b) ▦ Check your answers by working out all the calculations with a calculator. Key in 0.5 for $\frac{1}{2}$.

2. Use ⟨ partitioning ⟩ to help you answer these questions.

(a)  4.7 × 11

$= (4.7 \times 10) + (4.7 \times 1)$
$= \quad 47 \quad + \quad 4.7$
$= \quad\quad 51.7$

(b)  3.1 × 13

(c)  2.7 × 101

(d)  4.3 × 99

(e) 5.6 × 99

(f)  4.4 × 21

(g)  6.8 × 101

(h)  4.4 × 98

NOW TRY THIS!

● Are both these statements true? Explain your answer in words.

| $39 \times 3.6 = (40 \times 3.6) - (1 \times 3.6)$ | | $39 \div 3.6 = (40 \div 3.6) - (1 \div 3.6)$ |

● Write a similar problem and check whether it works.

Partitioning means splitting a number into parts (for example, $42 = 40 + 2$ or $42 = 21 + 21$). The **distributive law** for multiplication means that where two numbers are to be multiplied together, you can split one of them into parts, then multiply each part separately and add the results to get the answer: for example, $42 \times 3 = (40 \times 3) + (2 \times 3) = 120 + 6 = 126$.

Use the inverse

A Tina is doing some calculations on her calculator, but she keeps pressing the wrong keys! How can she undo the operation without pressing cancel and starting again? Write which keys she should press.

(a) 376 − 36 = | + | 3 | 6 | = |

(b) 376 ÷ 54 = | | | | |

(c) 376 + 79 = | | | |

(d) 376 − 47 = | | | | |

(e) 376 × 34 = | | | |

(f) 376 ÷ 62 = | | | | |

(g) 376 × 0.42 = | | | | | | | |

(h) $362 \times \frac{1}{4}$ = | | | | | | | | |

(i) $376 \times \frac{3}{5}$ = | | | | | | | | |

(j) $376 \times \frac{5}{7}$ = | | | | | | | | |

> You might not need to use all the boxes for your answers, or you might need to draw more.

!

B Use the inverse operation to check each calculation.

(a) 13 ÷ 4 = 3.25   *3.25 x 4 = (3 x 4) + (0.25 x 4) = 13* ✓

(b) 22.5 ÷ 4.25 = 6

(c) 23 × 8 = 168

(d) 1363 − 875 = 418

(e) 4.8 + 24.58 = 29.38

(f) 7.93 × 5 = 40.65

(g) 0.57 ÷ 6 = 0.095

 The **inverse** (or opposite) of addition is subtraction, and the **inverse** of multiplication is division. When you check the calculations in part B, make sure you use the inverse operations of the ones shown.

Developing Numeracy
Calculations
Year 7
© A & C BLACK

Use the inverse

C

1. Look at this number chain.

Input → − 6 → × 3 → + 2 → Output

(a) Input these numbers and write the outputs.

Input	7	8	10	13	14	15	26	27	36
Output	5								

(b) Now write the number chain in **reverse** to show how to return from the output number to the input number.

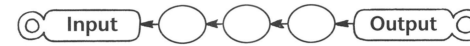

Input ← ◯ ← ◯ ← ◯ ← Output

(c) Check your answers to **(a)** and **(b)** by following your reverse number chain. Start with the output numbers in the table.

2. Write the **inverse** (reverse) of the number chains below. Fill in the outputs in the table, then use the inverse chain to check your answers.

(a)

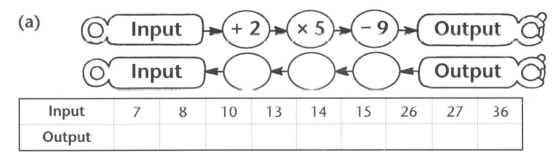

Input → + 2 → × 5 → − 9 → Output

Input ← ◯ ← ◯ ← ◯ ← Output

Input	7	8	10	13	14	15	26	27	36
Output									

(b)

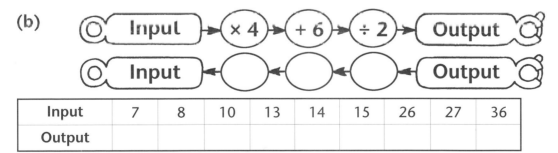

Input → × 4 → + 6 → ÷ 2 → Output

Input ← ◯ ← ◯ ← ◯ ← Output

Input	7	8	10	13	14	15	26	27	36
Output									

NOW TRY THIS!

- Use the inverse operations to help you solve these missing number questions. Start with the answer and work back through the question. Check your answers carefully.

  (a) (☐ − 4) × 2 = 12   **(b)** (☐ + 6) ÷ 5 = 8   **(c)** (☐ × 8) ÷ 4 + 1 = 13

- Make up three more missing number questions for a partner to solve.

The **inverse** (or opposite) of addition is subtraction, and the **inverse** of multiplication is division. To check your answers to the 'Now try this!' challenge, write the missing number in the original question and check that it makes the given answer.

Rapid facts

A **1.** Complete these number trios.

3^2 3×3 9

5^2 4^2

8^2 10^2

9^2 7^2

6^2 11^2

12^2 20^2

2. Use your answers to question 1 to help you complete these patterns.

(a) $0.1^2 =$ ___0.1___ × ___0.1___ = ___0.01___

$0.2^2 =$ ___0.2___ × ___0.2___ = ___0.04___

$0.3^2 =$ _____ × _____ = _____

$0.4^2 =$ _____ × _____ = _____

$0.5^2 =$ _____ × _____ = _____

$0.6^2 =$ _____ × _____ = _____

(b) $0.7^2 =$ _____ × _____ = _____

$0.8^2 =$ _____ × _____ = _____

$0.9^2 =$ _____ × _____ = _____

$1.0^2 =$ _____ × _____ = _____

$1.1^2 =$ _____ × _____ = _____

$1.2^2 =$ _____ × _____ = _____

B Join each │ square root │ question to its answer.

│ √8100 │ │ √49 │ │ √6400 │ │ √36 │ │ √0.25 │ │ √0.04 │ │ √0.16 │

│ 90 │ │ 80 │ │ 7 │ │ 0.2 │ │ 6 │ │ 0.4 │ │ 0.5 │

│ √100 │ │ √1 │ │ √0.01 │ │ √3600 │ │ √1.44 │ │ √0.09 │ │ √1.21 │

│ 0.1 │ │ 10 │ │ 60 │ │ 1 │ │ 0.3 │ │ 1.2 │ │ 1.1 │

 Remember that **squaring** and finding the **square root** are the inverse (or opposite) of each other, so a statement that gives a **square number** can be written the other way round as a square root: for example, $3^2 = 9$ and $\sqrt{9} = 3$.

Developing Numeracy
Calculations
Year 7
© A & C BLACK

C

1. Complete this crossnumber puzzle by working out the answers in your head.

1	0	6				

Across

1. $9^2 + 5^2$
3. $8^2 \times 2$
6. $2^2 + 400$
7. $10^2 \times 5$
8. $\sqrt{100}$
9. $9^2 + 4^2$
11. 8^2
13. $12^2 \times 2$
15. $4^2 - 1^2$
16. $8^2 - 4^2$
17. $\sqrt{1600}$
18. $4^2 - \sqrt{4}$
19. $\sqrt{400}$
20. $10^2 + 2^2 - 1^2$
21. 6^2
22. $\sqrt{36} + \sqrt{49}$
23. $\sqrt{144}$
25. $10^2 \times \sqrt{25}$
26. $\sqrt{100} \times 3^2$
27. $5^2 + 3^2$
28. $(5 + 5)^2 - 1^2$

Down

1. 4^2
2. $8^2 \times 10$
3. $10^2 + 7^2$
4. $8^2 + 5^2 - 2^2$
5. $10^2 + 10^2$
8. $9^2 + 8^2$
10. $6^2 \times 2$
11. $6^2 + 5^2$
12. 12^2
14. $10^2 - 4^2$
18. $11^2 + 10$
19. $11^2 + 12^2$
20. $12^2 + 5^2$
22. $10^2 + 3^2$
24. $\sqrt{144} + \sqrt{121}$

2. Answer these questions.

(a) $x^2 = 144$. What is x? _12_

(b) $n^2 = 1600$. What is n? ___

(c) $2 \times a^2 = 50$. What is a? ___

(d) $2 \times b^2 = 18$. What is b? ___

(e) $c^2 \div 2 = 8$. What is c? ___

(f) $y^2 \times 5 = 5$. What is y? ___

● Make up four questions of your own, using the letters p, q, r and s.

If a square or square root question involves another operation (such as multiplying), always work out the square or square root first: for example, $7^2 \times 3 = 49 \times 3 = 147$.

BODMAS

A

The word | BODMAS | can help you to remember the order of operations.

B
Brackets
Do brackets first.

O
Other
Do other things such as squares, roots and powers.

DM
Division and Multiplication
Do these next.

AS
Addition and Subtraction
Do these last.

Answer these questions using the order of BODMAS. Underline the part of the question you do first.

(a) $\underline{4 \times 2} + 5 =$ _13_

(b) $3 + 10 \times 6 =$ _____

(c) $(4 + 9) \times 2 =$ _____

(d) $16 \div 4 + 4 =$ _____

(e) $27 \div 3 + 6 =$ _____

(f) $14 \div (9 - 2) =$ _____

(g) $20 - 16 \div 2$ _____

(h) $14 - 8 \div 2 =$ _____

(i) $(15 - 6) \div 3 =$ _____

(j) $(3 + 4) \times 5 + 1 =$ _____

(k) $5 \times (4 - 2) =$ _____

(l) $(4 + 6) \times (15 - 12) =$ _____

(m) $3 + 4^2 =$ _____

(n) $(5 + 1)^2 =$ _____

(o) $3 \times \sqrt{25} =$ _____

B

If all the operations in a question are the same, work from left to right.

$$24 \div 6 \div 2 = ?$$

The answer is 2 (not 8).

Tick the true statements and correct the false ones.

(a) $3 + 6 + 9 = 18$ ✔

(b) $13 + 5 + 12 = \cancel{29}\ 30$

(c) $8 + 7 + 11 = 26$

(d) $18 + 4 + 24 = 46$

(e) $6 + 3 + 5 + 8 = 23$

(f) $15 + 8 + 17 + 9 = 49$

(g) $18 - 6 - 4 = 8$

(h) $23 - 5 - 17 = 2$

(i) $16 - 7 - 8 = {}^-1$

(j) $13 - 11 - 4 = {}^-2$

(k) $23 - 12 - 5 - 6 = 0$

(l) $19 - 4 - 8 - 3 - 2 = 2$

(m) $12 \div 6 \div 2 = 2$

(n) $18 \div 3 \div 3 = 18$

(o) $24 \div 8 \div 4 = 12$

(p) $36 \div 2 \div 9 = 2$

(q) $64 \div 8 \div 4 \div 2 = 1$

(r) $64 \div 2 \div 16 \div 4 = 4$

(s) $3 \times 5 \times 6 = 90$

(t) $2 \times 8 \times 5 = 80$

(u) $7 \times 4 \times 3 = 84$

 Don't worry if a calculation has only some of the operations of BODMAS. Just continue to follow the order of BODMAS, leaving out any operations that are missing: for example, $100 - 25 \times 3 + (7 + 4) = 36$.

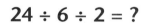
3rd   2nd   4th   1st

Developing Numeracy
Calculations
Year 7
© A & C BLACK

BODMAS

C 1.

When a calculation has a division line, write brackets around what is above and below the line. Work them out before you divide.

$$\frac{4 + 8}{8 - 2} = \frac{(4 + 8)}{(8 - 2)} = \frac{12}{6} = 2$$

(a) $\dfrac{5 + 13}{4 + 2}$ $= \dfrac{(5 + 13)}{(4 + 2)} = \dfrac{18}{6} = 3$

(b) $\dfrac{8 + 12}{4 + 6}$ = _____

(c) $\dfrac{16 - 10}{9 - 3}$ = _____

(d) $\dfrac{4 \times 5}{10 \div 2}$ = _____

(e) $\dfrac{5 + 9}{2}$ = _____

(f) $\dfrac{18 - 3}{5}$ = _____

(g) $\dfrac{48}{12 \div 4}$ = _____

(h) $\dfrac{100}{4 \times 5}$ = _____

(i) $\dfrac{5 + 11}{2 \times 2} + 7 = \dfrac{(5 + 11)}{(2 \times 2)} + 7 = \dfrac{16}{4} + 7 = 4 + 7 = 11$

(j) $\dfrac{15 - 7}{12 \div 3} - 1$ = _____

(k) $\dfrac{3 \times 9}{21 - 18} \times 3$ = _____

2.  Try both of these methods for each question. Do you get the same answer?

Work out the top and bottom first, write down the answers and then divide.

Use the brackets keys and key in the whole question.

(a) $\dfrac{34 + 76}{64 - 53}$ _____

(b) $\dfrac{15 \times 16}{3 \times 40}$ _____

(c) $\dfrac{812 - 346}{189 + 44}$ _____

(d) $\dfrac{91 - 49}{84 \div 4}$ _____

(e) $\dfrac{18 \times 32.5}{52 - 13}$ _____

(f) $\dfrac{712 \div 16}{11.125 \times 2}$ _____

NOW TRY THIS!

● If $a = 4$, find the values of:

Remember to work out squares and square roots before division, multiplication, addition and subtraction.

!

(a) $3a^2$

(b) $5a^2 - 2$

(c) $\dfrac{\sqrt{a}}{2}$

(d) $\dfrac{3 \times \sqrt{a}}{6}$

(e) $\dfrac{a^2}{\sqrt{a}}$

(f) $\dfrac{a^2 - 7a + 3}{\sqrt{a} + 4}$

 Always look carefully at a calculation and think of BODMAS to see which order to solve it in.

Rapid recall

1. Each line of this star shows an instruction.

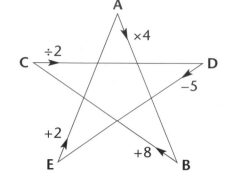

(a) Start at **A** with the number **10**. Move in alphabetical order around the star doing the calculations until you return to **A**. What is your finish number? _____

(b) Now start at **B** with the number **10** and return to **B**. What is your finish number? _____

(c) Find the finish numbers if you start with **10** at:

C _____   D _____   E _____

2. In the same way, complete the table for each star, starting at each letter with the number **6**.

(a)

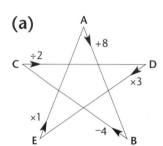

Starting letter	Finish number
A	
B	
C	
D	
E	

(b)

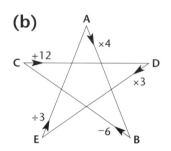

Starting letter	Finish number
A	
B	
C	
D	
E	

3. Work out the answers in your head. Colour the odd one out in each set of three.

(a) | double 3.6 | 10 − 3.8 | 1.9 + 4.3 |

(b) | 1.6 × 20 | half 32 | 4 × 8 |

(c) | 670 ÷ 100 | $8^2 + 1$ | half 13.4 |

(d) | 50 − 68 | half 36 | 6 × ⁻3 |

(e) | 1 − 0.62 | 0.19 × 2 | 0.2 × 19 |

(f) | 5.6 ÷ 7 | 1 − 0.02 | 7.2 ÷ 9 |

B

Join the questions to the correct answers.

| 400 × 0.8 | 0.04 × 0.8 | 0.4 × 8 | 4 × 0.8 | 40 × 0.8 |

| **320** | **32** | **3.2** | **0.32** | **0.032** |

Use 4 × 8 = 32 to help you. **!**

| 0.4 × 80 | 0.4 × 0.8 | 4 × 8 | 0.04 × 8 | 4 × 0.08 |

All the questions on this page should be solved in your head, but you can jot down notes on a separate piece of paper if you need to. Remember that when two numbers being multiplied are both made 10 times larger, the answer will be 100 times larger (for example, 4 × 8 = 32 and 40 × 80 = 3200).

C Every book has its own ISBN (identification number) made from ten digits. To check whether an ISBN is genuine, you can follow these rules.

Multiply the first digit by 10, the next by 9, the next by 8, and so on. Add up all the answers and divide the total by 11. If your answer is **not** a whole number then the digits are **not** a genuine ISBN.

Example:

0	1	2	5	0	9	2	5	6	3
×10	×9	×8	×7	×6	×5	×4	×3	×2	×1

$0 + 9 + 16 + 35 + 0 + 45 + 8 + 15 + 12 + 3 = 143$, $143 ÷ 11 = 13$

So this is a genuine ISBN.

1. Put a cross beside the numbers which are **not** genuine ISBNs. Show your workings.

(a)

1	2	0	7	2	4	5	3	7	2
×10	×9	×8	×7	×6	×5	×4	×3	×2	×1

(b)

3	5	5	0	6	2	8	1	5	6
×10	×9	×8	×7	×6	×5	×4	×3	×2	×1

(c)

0	3	3	5	0	9	3	6	6	3
×10	×9	×8	×7	×6	×5	×4	×3	×2	×1

(d)

1	7	6	6	2	4	9	8	0	1
×10	×9	×8	×7	×6	×5	×4	×3	×2	×1

(e)

1	8	9	9	7	1	2	2	4	0
×10	×9	×8	×7	×6	×5	×4	×3	×2	×1

10 + 18 +

2. Now find any book. Write the ISBN and check whether the rule works.

×10	×9	×8	×7	×6	×5	×4	×3	×2	×1

NOW TRY THIS!

● If $a = 9$, $b = 18$ and $c = 10$, find the values of:

(a) $a + b$ _____

(b) $b - a$ _____

(c) $\dfrac{b}{a}$ _____

(d) a^2 _____

(e) $b × c$ _____

(f) $a × c ÷ b$ _____

(g) $\dfrac{b}{a} + c^2$ _____

(h) $a^2 + c^2 - b$ _____

 ISBN stands for International Standard Book Number. When you are checking the ISBNs, do the multiplications in your head. Find strategies that help you to add up the numbers (for example, group numbers that add up to multiples of 10). You might find it useful to write a list of multiples of 11 to help you check the totals.

Mental measurements

A

1. The diagram shows how to convert centimetres to metres, and vice versa.

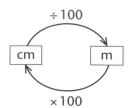

Use the diagram to help you convert these measurements.

(a) 4 m = _400_ cm   **(b)** 300 cm = _____ m   **(c)** 12 m = _____ cm

(d) 170 cm = _____ m   **(e)** 4.5 m = _____ cm   **(f)** 325 cm = _____ m

(g) 0.75 m = _____ cm   **(h)** 0.04 m = _____ cm   **(i)** 17 cm = _____ m

2. Complete the diagrams to show how to convert these units of measurement.

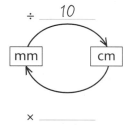

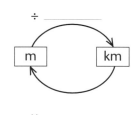

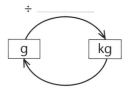

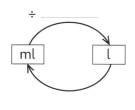

3. Use the diagrams to help you convert these measurements.

(a) 3.4 cm = _____ mm   **(b)** 465 mm = _____ cm

(c) 4600 m = _____ km   **(d)** 2.84 km = _____ m

(e) 63 kg = _____ g   **(f)** 460 g = _____ kg

(g) 0.67 kg = _____ g   **(h)** 5275 g = _____ kg

(i) 6.5 l = _____ ml   **(j)** 4880 ml = _____ l

(k) 7.284 l = _____ ml   **(l)** 34 ml = _____ l

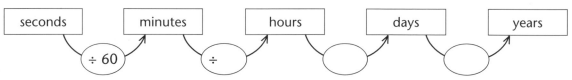

B

1. Complete this diagram.

> Use the number of days in a normal year. **!**

| seconds | | minutes | | hours | | days | | years |

÷ 60   ÷ _____

2. Use the diagram to help you convert these measurements.

(a) 180 seconds = _____ minutes   **(b)** 480 hours = _____ days

(c) 730 days = _____ years   **(d)** 4 minutes = _____ seconds

(e) 2 days = _____ hours   **(f)** 12 hours = _____ minutes

 When you multiply a positive number by 10, 100 or 1000, the digits move to the **left** to make the number larger (for example, 2.67 × 10 = 26.7). When you divide a positive number by 10, 100 or 1000, the digits move to the **right** to make the number smaller (for example, 348 ÷ 100 = 3.48).

Mental measurements

C

w

l ▢ *l*

w

You can calculate the perimeter and area of a rectangle
using these formulae:

Perimeter = 2*l* + 2*w* = 2(*l* + *w*) | Area = *l* × *w*

> The photos are not
> drawn to scale.

!

1. Calculate mentally the perimeter and area of each photo.

(a)  4 cm
8 cm

Perimeter = ___24 cm___

Area   = ___32 cm²___

(b)   5 cm
9 cm

Perimeter = _____

Area   = _____

(c) 7 cm
4 cm

Perimeter = _____

Area   = _____

(d) 4 cm
5 cm

Perimeter = _____

Area   = _____

(e)  10 cm
12 cm

Perimeter = _____

Area   = _____

(f)  7 cm
11 cm

Perimeter = _____

Area   = _____

(g) 12 cm
9 cm

Perimeter = _____

Area   = _____

(h) 12 cm
12 cm

Perimeter = _____

Area   = _____

(i)  7 cm
21 cm

Perimeter = _____

Area   = _____

2. Work out lengths and widths of rectangles with these perimeters and areas.

(a) Perimeter = 26 cm
Area   = 40 cm²

Length   = ____ cm

Width   = ____ cm

(b) Perimeter = 30 cm
Area   = 50 cm²

Length   = ____ cm

Width   = ____ cm

(c) Perimeter = 28 cm
Area   = 13 cm²

Length   = ____ cm

Width   = ____ cm

NOW TRY THIS!

● Find the area of each of the triangles A, B, C and D
if the side of the square is:

(a) 6 cm   **(b)** 10 cm   **(c)** 7 cm

 For the 'Now try this!' challenge, the area of a triangle can be written as
the formula $\frac{1}{2} \times l \times w$. Sometimes the length (*l*) and width (*w*) are known
as base (*b*) and perpendicular height (*h*), so the formula can also be written
as $\frac{1}{2} \times b \times h$.

Amazing strategies

1. Answer these doubling and halving questions. How quickly can you complete the maze?

Time yourself!

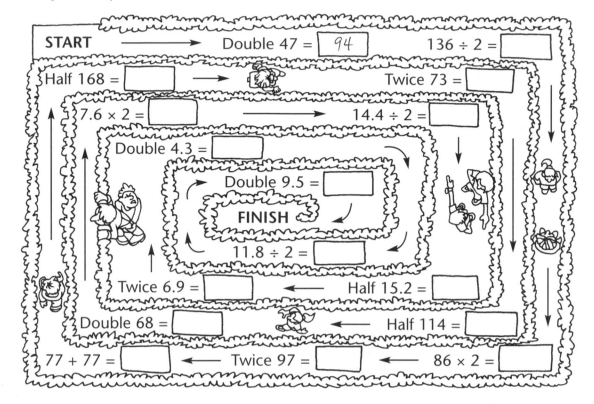

START → Double 47 = [94]   136 ÷ 2 = [ ]

Half 168 = [ ] →   Twice 73 = [ ]

7.6 × 2 = [ ] →   14.4 ÷ 2 = [ ]

Double 4.3 = [ ]

Double 9.5 = [ ]

FINISH

11.8 ÷ 2 = [ ]

Twice 6.9 = [ ] ←   Half 15.2 = [ ]

Double 68 = [ ]   Half 114 = [ ]

77 + 77 = [ ] ←   Twice 97 = [ ] ←   86 × 2 = [ ]

2. Describe how you would use doubling to answer these questions.

(a) 47 + 48 = ___95___

This is one more than double 47. Double 47 = 94, and 94 + 1 = 95.

(b) 73 + 74 = _____

(c) 68 + 67 = _____

(d) 85 + 86 = _____

B Shade the correct answer for each question.

(a) 7.8 + 7.9 | 15.7 | 15.5 | 14.7 | **(b)** 8.6 + 8.7 | 16.13 | 17.5 | 17.3 |

(c) 6.7 + 6.8 | 13.3 | 12.5 | 13.5 | **(d)** 9.5 + 9.6 | 19.2 | 19.1 | 18.2 |

(e) 5.9 + 5.8 | 11.8 | 11.7 | 12.1 | **(f)** 7.7 + 7.6 | 14.1 | 14.3 | 15.3 |

These calculations will be easier if you know by heart doubles of numbers to 100. If you don't, you can find the answers by splitting the number to be doubled into tens and units (for example, 47 = 40 + 7), then double each part and add the two together.

Developing Numeracy
Calculations
Year 7
© A & C BLACK

Amazing strategies

C

1. Fill in the missing number. Then write three related facts to give two addition statements and two subtraction statements.

(a) | 4.6 + [4.7] = 9.3 | 4.7 + 4.6 = 9.3 | 9.3 – 4.6 = 4.7 | 9.3 – 4.7 = 4.6

(b) | 5.6 + [ ] = 11.1 | | |

(c) | 9.8 + [ ] = 19.5 | | |

(d) | 8.7 – [ ] = 4.4 | | |

(e) | 15.7 – [ ] = 7.8 | | |

2.

(a) Two identical tickets together cost £17.60. How much does one ticket cost?

(b) What number do you add to 4.9 to get to 9.7?

(c) A pen costs 68p. If you buy two, how much change will you get from £2?

(d) A TV costing £147 is reduced to half price. How much does it cost in the sale?

(e) Jo had £17.30. She bought a CD and had £8.70 left. How much did the CD cost?

(f) If two people share 173p equally, what is the most each can have?

(g) Two items cost £495 and £506. What is the total cost?

(h) A battery costs 88p and a rubber costs 66p. If you buy two of each, how much change will you get from £5?

NOW TRY THIS!

● Use doubling to help you answer these questions.

(a) 426 + 388 = *(400 x 2) + 26 – 12 = 814*

(b) 319 + 294 = _____

(c) 651 + 648 = _____

You can add and subtract decimals in the same way as whole numbers. Just remember that decimals are 10 (or 100 or 1000...) times smaller than whole numbers: for example, 14.7 is 10 times smaller than 147.

Jump to it!

A Complete the diagrams to help you add these pairs of numbers. First add the nearest multiple of 100, then adjust.

(a) 440 + 285 = _725_

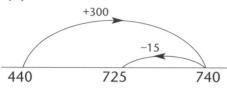

440   725   740

(b) 560 + 391 = _____

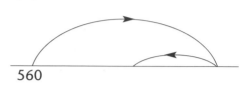

560

(c) 376 + 187 = _____

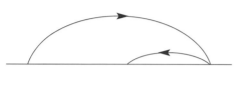

(d) 477 + 276 = _____

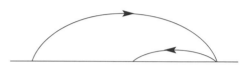

(e) 426 + 696 = _____

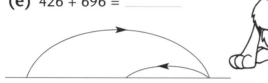

(f) 272 + 567 = _____

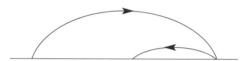

B Complete the diagrams to help you subtract these pairs of numbers. First subtract the nearest multiple of 100, then adjust.

(a) 440 − 285 = _155_

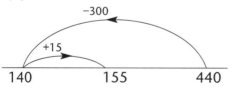

140   155   440

(b) 560 − 391 = _____

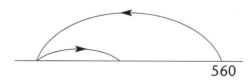

560

(c) 376 − 187 = _____

(d) 477 − 276 = _____

(e) 831 − 172 = _____

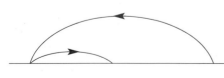

(f) 665 − 488 = _____

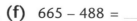

When you are adding and subtracting numbers mentally, it is often easier first to add near multiples of 10, 100 or 1000 and then to adjust the answer. Think carefully about whether to add or subtract when you adjust the answer.

Developing Numeracy
Calculations
Year 7
© A & C BLACK

Jump to it!

C

1. Draw diagrams to help you add or subtract these pairs of decimals. First add or subtract the nearest whole number, then adjust.

(a) 4.7 + 2.9 = _7.6_

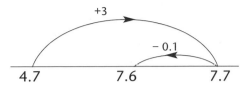

(b) 5.7 + 3.9 = _____

(c) 8.6 + 6.8 = _____

(d) 9.4 – 4.9 = _____

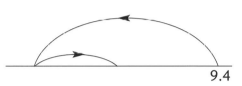

(e) 14.6 – 5.8 = _____

(f) 5.36 – 1.99 = _____

2. Now try answering these questions **without** drawing diagrams. First add or subtract the nearest whole number, then adjust.

(a) 3.5 + 4.9 = _8.4_   **(b)** 6.7 + 5.9 = _____   **(c)** 5.7 + 9.8 = _____

(d) 13.4 + 1.8 = _____   **(e)** 17.4 + 3.8 = _____   **(f)** 36.5 + 2.9 = _____

(g) 8.52 + 4.99 = _____   **(h)** 6.11 + 7.99 = _____   **(i)** 4.33 + 9.98 = _____

(j) 3.5 – 1.9 – _____   **(k)** 6.7 – 3.9 = _____   **(l)** 15.7 – 9.8 = _____

(m) 13.4 – 1.8 = _____   **(n)** 17.4 – 3.8 = _____   **(o)** 36.5 – 2.9 = _____

(p) 8.52 – 4.99 = _____   **(q)** 6.11 – 2.99 = _____   **(r)** 14.33 – 9.98 = _____

NOW TRY THIS!

● List the different amounts you could spend if you bought any two of these items.

Use the same method that you used to answer question C2.

£13.99

£6.98

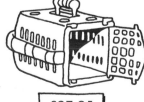

£27.95

£16.90

When you are adding and subtracting numbers mentally, it is often easier first to add near multiples of 10, 100 or 1000 and then to adjust the answer. Think carefully about whether to add or subtract when you adjust the answer.

**Developing Numeracy
Calculations
Year 7**
© A & C BLACK

27

Parting ways

A

1. Choose two cards and find the total. Use **partitioning** and show your working.

 78   95   166   147   86   69   283   74   356

(a) [86] + [78] = 164 | 86 + 78   80 + 70 = 150
6 + 8 = 14
164

(b) ☐ + ☐ = _____

(c) ☐ + ☐ = _____

(d) ☐ + ☐ = _____

(e) ☐ + ☐ = _____

(f) ☐ + ☐ = _____

(g) ☐ + ☐ = _____

2. On another piece of paper, write subtractions to check your answers.

B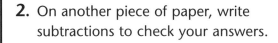

Use partitioning to answer these questions. You do not need to show your working.

(a) 467 + 27 = _____   **(b)** 148 + 36 = _____   **(c)** 235 + 64 = _____

(d) 373 + 45 = _____   **(e)** 283 + 64 = _____   **(f)** 654 + 57 = _____

(g) 269 + 44 = _____   **(h)** 467 + 34 = _____   **(i)** 595 + 28 = _____

(j) 881 + 62 = _____   **(k)** 328 + 73 = _____   **(l)** 874 + 61 = _____

 Partitioning means splitting a number into parts (for example, 142 = 100 + 40 + 2). It is often useful to split numbers into hundreds, tens and units like this, particularly when adding. Add each part separately, then find the total of the parts.

Developing Numeracy
Calculations
Year 7
© A & C BLACK

Parting ways

1. Play this game with a partner. You each need a coloured pencil and scrap paper.

☆ Take turns to choose one number from each wrestler and write them on a separate piece of paper. Choose your numbers carefully!

☆ Find the difference between the two numbers by counting on from the smaller number. Record your answer.

☆ If your answer is on the grid, colour it in your colour.

☆ The winner is the first player to colour four numbers in a line.

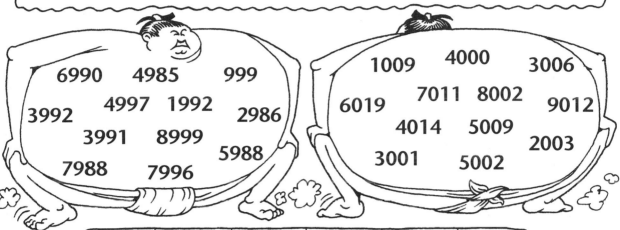

6990	4985	999
4997	1992	
3992		2986
3991	8999	
	5988	
7988	7996	

1009	4000	3006
7011	8002	9012
6019		
4014	5009	2003
3001	5002	

5	6	8	9	10	11
12	13	14	15	17	20
21	22	23	24	31	1004
1009	1010	1011	1012	1014	1016
1018	1020	1022	1023	1024	1028
2002	2014	2016	2019	2020	2023

2. Look at your recordings. Check all your answers using addition.

● Find the differences in price between pairs of items.

£4.98

£6.92

£12.08

£9.06

In the grid game, your lines can be horizontal, vertical or diagonal. Find the difference by counting on from the smaller number to the larger number (you will find it easiest if you choose the smaller number from the wrestler on the left and the larger number from the wrestler on the right). Think which multiples of 1000 lie between the two numbers.

Factor fiction?

A

1. Use ⬚factors to help you answer these questions mentally.

(a) 4.2 × 30

4.2 × 10 × 3

42 x 3 = 126

(b) 3.5 × 20

3.5 × 10 × ____

_____ =

(c) 7.3 × 30

____ × 10 ×

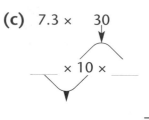

_____ =

(d) 3.2 × 40

3.2 × ____ × ____

_____ =

(e) 2.1 × 60

2.1 × ____ × ____

_____ =

(f) 5.3 × 30

____ × ____ × ____

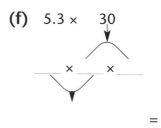

_____ =

(g) 1.8 × 40

____ × ____ × ____

_____ =

(h) 8.4 × 20

____ × ____ × ____

_____ =

(i) 9.2 × 30

____ × ____ × ____

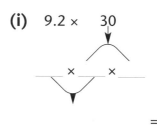

_____ =

B

1. Use factors to help you answer these questions mentally.

(a) 96 ÷ 6

96 ÷ 3 ÷ 2

32 ÷ 2 = 16

(b) 280 ÷ 8

280 ÷ 4 ÷ 2

_____ ÷ 2 =

(c) 150 ÷ 6

150 ÷ 3 ÷ 2

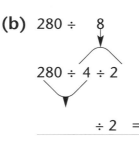

_____ ÷ 2 =

(d) 192 ÷ 6

192 ÷ 3 ÷ 2

_____ ÷ 2 =

(e) 440 ÷ 8

440 ÷ 4 ÷ 2

_____ ÷ 2 =

(f) 486 ÷ 9

486 ÷ 3 ÷ 3

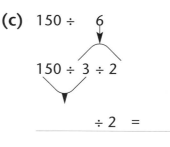
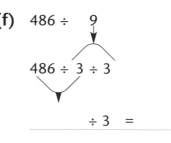

_____ ÷ 3 =

2. Use factors to help you answer these questions mentally.

(a) 248 ÷ 8 = _____

(b) 426 ÷ 6 = _____

(c) 342 ÷ 9 = _____

(d) 512 ÷ 8 = _____

(e) 488 ÷ 8 = _____

(f) 696 ÷ 12 = _____

A **factor** is a number that divides exactly into another without a remainder (for example, 2 and 3 are both factors of 6, and 2 and 4 are both factors of 8).

**Developing Numeracy
Calculations
Year 7**
© A & C BLACK

Factor fiction?

1.

Multiplying any number by 5 or 50 is easy! Just multiply by 10 or 100 and halve the answer.

Use this method to answer the questions.

(a) 42 × 5 = _210_

(b) 62 × 5 = _____

(c) 68 × 5 = _____

(d) 82 × 5 = _____

(e) 86 × 5 = _____

(f) 88 × 5 = _____

(g) 57 × 5 = _____

(h) 69 × 5 = _____

(i) 77 × 5 = _____

(j) 24 × 50 = _____

(k) 36 × 50 = _____

(l) 44 × 50 = _____

(m) 66 × 50 = _____

(n) 84 × 50 = _____

(o) 88 × 50 = _____

(p) 31 × 50 = _____

(q) 37 × 50 = _____

(r) 55 × 50 = _____

2.

When multiplying two numbers, if you double one and halve the other you get the same answer.

Example:

$$35 \times 8 = 280$$

double   halve

$$70 \times 4 = 280$$

Use this doubling and halving method to answer the questions.

(a) 15 × 8 = _____

(b) 25 × 6 = _____

(c) 35 × 6 = _____

(d) 45 × 4 = _____

(e) 45 × 6 = _____

(f) 15 × 12 = _____

(g) 35 × 12 = _____

(h) 15 × 16 = _____

(i) 45 × 8 = _____

(j) 3.5 × 8 = _____

(k) 2.5 × 16 = _____

(l) 3.5 × 18 = _____

(m) 25 × 18 = _____

(n) 4.5 × 12 = _____

(o) 0.4 × 14 = _____

NOW TRY THIS!

● Explain why the doubling and halving method works.

_____

_____

_____

When you use the doubling and halving method, it doesn't matter which number you double and which you halve.

Developing Numeracy
Calculations
Year 7
© A & C BLACK

31

Super strategies

A

1. Use **partitioning** to help you solve these word problems.

(a) A rectangle has a width of 7.3 cm and a length of 12 cm. What is its area?

$87.6 \ cm^2$

$7.3 \times 12 =$	7×12	84
	0.3×12	$+ \ 3.6$
		87.6

(b) A rectangle has an area of 330 cm² and a width of 15 cm. What is its length?

$330 \div 15 = 300 \div 15$
$ 30 \div 15$

(c) One bottle of shampoo costs £5.70. How much do 12 bottles cost?

_____

$£5.70 \times 12$

(d) A set meal for four people costs £43 in total. How much should each person pay? _____

$£43 \div 4$

(e) If one pound (£) is worth 1.6 euros, how many euros is £27 worth?

(f) Nine bags of crisps cost £4.05. How much does each bag cost?

(g) A regular 14-sided polygon has sides 6.2 cm long. What is its perimeter?

(h) If one pound (£) is worth 1.5 US dollars, how many pounds are 12 US dollars worth? _____

B

Fill in the missing number. Then write three related facts to give two multiplication statements and two division statements.

(a) $4.5 \times 7 =$	31.5	$7 \times 4.5 = 31.5$	$31.5 \div 7 = 4.5$	$31.5 \div 4.5 = 7$
(b) $5.6 \times 4 =$				
(c) $9.8 \times 5 =$				
(d) $15.4 \div 7 =$				
(e) $18.4 \div 8 =$				

Partitioning means splitting a number into parts (for example, 5.8 = 5 + 0.8). In multiplication, you can split either number: for example, to calculate 4.2 × 12 you can split the 12 into 10 and 2 **or** the 4.2 into 4 and 0.2. In division, you must always split the number which is being divided: for example, to find 128 ÷ 4, split the 128 into 100 and 28.

Developing Numeracy
Calculations
Year 7
© A & C BLACK

Super strategies

1. You can use **partitioning** to help you multiply by 11. Answer these questions using partitioning.

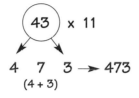

Example: 43 × 11 = 43 × 10   430
                    + 43 × 1   + 43
                    ─────────────────
                                 473

(a) 34 × 11 = _____   **(b)** 54 × 11 = _____   **(c)** 63 × 11 = _____

2.

To multiply a two-digit number by 11, write the two digits as the first and last digits of the answer. Then add them and write the total in between them.

Example:

 × 11

4   7   3 → 473
  (4 + 3)

(a) Test this method on some other two-digit numbers.

◯ × 11   ◯ × 11   ◯ × 11   ◯ × 11

_____   _____   _____   _____

(b) Does this method work for all two-digit numbers? _____

Try these: 38 × 11   47 × 11   59 × 11

                _____   _____   _____

(c) Write an extra rule so that the method works for all two-digit numbers.

_____

_____

_____

NOW TRY THIS!

● Arrange the numbers 1, 2, 3, 4, 6, 8, 12 and 24 in the circles so that each multiplication question gives the answer 24.

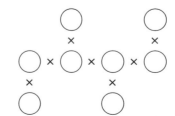

 Partitioning means splitting a number into parts (for example, 5.8 = 5 + 0.8). In multiplication, you can split either number: for example, to calculate 4.2 × 12 you can split the 12 into 10 and 2 **or** the 4.2 into 4 and 0.2. In division, you must always split the number which is being divided: for example, to find 128 ÷ 4, split the 128 into 100 and 28.

Developing Numeracy
Calculations
Year 7
© A & C BLACK

33

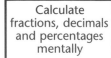

Get a head start

A These diagrams show how you can find percentages of a number in your head.

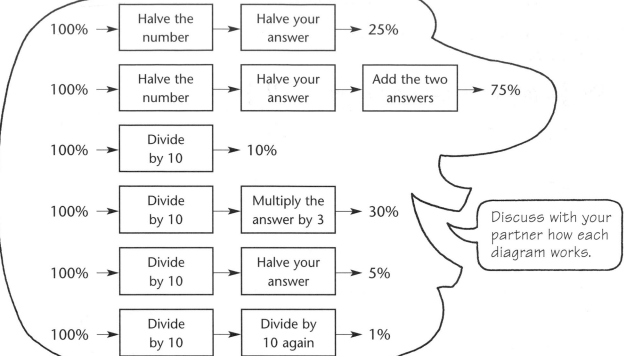

100% → Halve the number → Halve your answer → 25%

100% → Halve the number → Halve your answer → Add the two answers → 75%

100% → Divide by 10 → 10%

100% → Divide by 10 → Multiply the answer by 3 → 30%

100% → Divide by 10 → Halve your answer → 5%

100% → Divide by 10 → Divide by 10 again → 1%

Discuss with your partner how each diagram works.

Use the diagrams above to help you answer these questions mentally.

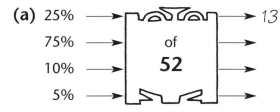

(a) 25% → *13*
75% → of **52**
10% →
5% →

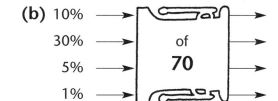

(b) 10% →
30% → of **70**
5% →
1% →

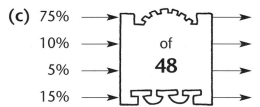

(c) 75% →
10% → of **48**
5% →
15% →

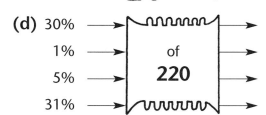

(d) 30% →
1% → of **220**
5% →
31% →

B Complete these rows of ⬚ equivalent ⬚ percentages, decimals and fractions.

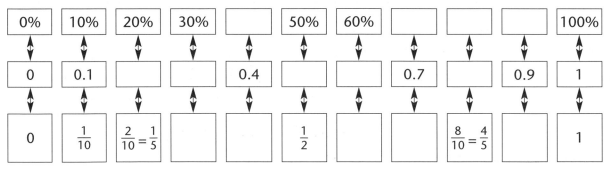

0%	10%	20%	30%		50%	60%				100%
0	0.1		0.4			0.7		0.9		1
0	$\frac{1}{10}$	$\frac{2}{10}=\frac{1}{5}$			$\frac{1}{2}$			$\frac{8}{10}=\frac{4}{5}$		1

Equivalent means equal (for example, 50% is equivalent to 0.5 and $\frac{1}{2}$). You will find it useful to learn by heart the fraction, decimal and percentage equivalents in part B. Give the fractions in their simplest form.

Developing Numeracy
Calculations
Year 7
© A & C BLACK

Get a head start

$\frac{1}{5} = 0.2 = 20\%$ $\frac{1}{4} = 0.25 = 25\%$ $\frac{1}{8}$ is half of $\frac{1}{4}$

1. Use the facts above to help you answer the questions. Write each fraction as a decimal, then as a percentage.

(a) $\frac{2}{5}$ = $(0.2 \times 2 = 0.4)$ = 0.4 = 40%   **(b)** $\frac{3}{5}$ = _____

(c) $\frac{4}{5}$ = _____   **(d)** $\frac{3}{4}$ = _____

(e) $\frac{1}{8}$ = _____   **(f)** $\frac{3}{8}$ = _____

2. (a) $\frac{1}{4}$ of a number is 24. What is $\frac{1}{8}$ of this number? _____

(b) $\frac{1}{8}$ of a number is 5. What is $\frac{1}{4}$ of this number? _____

3. Write how many grams of fat are in each bag of crisps.

(a)   20% fat   CRISPS   55 g   *11 y*

(b)   10% fat   CRISPS   75 g

(c)   5% fat   CRISPS   120 g

(d)   15% fat   CRISPS   95 g

(e)   1% fat   CRISPS   150 g

(f)   11% fat   CRISPS   80 y

4. Complete these facts. Write the **equivalent** fractions and decimals.

(a) 1% = $\frac{1}{100}$ = 0.01   **(b)** 3% =   =   **(c)** 7% =   =

(d) 19% =   =   **(e)** 23% =   =   **(f)** 79% =   =

NOW TRY THIS!

● Find the total of each row and column in the grid.
● Use your answers to find the total of all the numbers in the grid. _____

$\frac{1}{2}$	0.125	$\frac{1}{8}$	$\frac{3}{4}$
0.25	$\frac{1}{2}$	0.75	
$\frac{3}{4}$	$\frac{5}{8}$	$\frac{1}{4}$	

● Make another fraction square for a partner to solve.

💡 **Equivalent** means equal (for example, 50% is equivalent to 0.5 and $\frac{1}{2}$). In the 'Now try this!' challenge, do not add together all your answers to find the overall total, as this will mean that each number is included twice. Add **either** the row numbers **or** the column numbers (and use the other set to check your answers).

Best estimates

A Look at the calculation on each rugby ball. Tick the estimate you think is the best from those listed beneath. Work out all the answers to see if you are correct.

(a) (7.5 × 2.5)

✓ 7 × 3
   7 × 2
   8 × 2
   8 × 3

7.5 × 2.5 = 18.75

(b) (8.5 × 3.5)

8 × 3
8 × 4
9 × 3
9 × 4

(c) (45 × 25)

40 × 20
40 × 30
50 × 20
50 × 30

(d) (35 × 65)

40 × 60
40 × 70
30 × 60
30 × 70

(e) (5.5 × 4.5)

6 × 5
5 × 4
5 × 5
6 × 4

(f) (8.5 × 15)

8 × 20
8 × 10
9 × 10
9 × 20

(g) (12.5 × 3.5)

12 × 3
12 × 4
13 × 4
13 × 3

(h) (14.5 × 5.5)

14 × 5
15 × 5
15 × 6
14 × 6

(i) (75 × 45)

70 × 40
80 × 40
80 × 50
70 × 50

(j) (17.5 × 2.5)

17 × 3
17 × 2
18 × 2
18 × 3

(k) (7.5 × 11.5)

8 × 11
7 × 12
8 × 12
9 × 11

B For each calculation write an estimate first, then find the exact answer.

(a) 16.5 × 4.5 =   Estimate: _____   Exact answer: _____

(b) 10.2 × 3.5 =   Estimate: _____   Exact answer: _____

(c) 14.8 × 12.2 =   Estimate: _____   Exact answer: _____

(d) 32 × 17.8 =   Estimate: _____   Exact answer: _____

 Making an estimate before doing a calculation gives you a good idea of what the answer might be. It will help you to spot if you have made a mistake.

Best estimates

C

1. Tick the best approximation for each question.

(a) | 30.8 + 19.6

 308 + 196    ✓ 31 + 20   30 + 19    31 + 19

(b) | 416 − 234

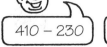 410 − 230   420 − 230   400 − 250   41.6 − 23.4

(c) | 5.82 × 4.57

 582 x 457   5 x 5   6 x 4   6 x 5

(d) | 3684 + 6039

 4000 + 6000    3500 + 6000    370 + 6000   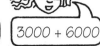 3000 + 6000

(e) | 48.3 × 5.62

 48 x 56   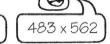 483 x 562   50 x 5    50 x 6

(f) | 54.8 ÷ 12.7

 60 ÷ 12   60 ÷ 13   50 ÷ 12   50 ÷ 13

(g) | 7632 − 4398

 8000 − 4000   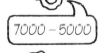 7000 − 5000   7.6 − 4.3    8000 − 5000

(h) | 432 ÷ 19

 400 ÷ 10   500 ÷ 20   400 ÷ 20   500 ÷ 10

(i) | 86.3 − 48.2

 80 − 40   90 − 50   90 − 40   80 − 50

2. Discuss each answer with a partner and explain your reasoning.

NOW TRY THIS!

A _____↓_____ B

● Estimate the number the arrow is pointing to, if:

(a) A = 0 and B = 2 _____

(b) A = 7 and B = 20 _____

(c) A = ⁻6 and B = 4 _____

(d) A = 0.4 and B = 1.6 _____

 For the 'Now try this!' challenge, you might find it helpful to split the line into equal parts.

**Developing Numeracy
Calculations
Year 7**
© A & C BLACK

37

Line 'em up

A

Write the missing digits in these addition and subtraction questions.

(a)
```
  2 3 5
+ 6 7 8
───────
  9 1 3
  1 1
```

(b)
```
  5 □ 4
+ 1 8 3
───────
  □ 1 7
```

(c)
```
  2 3 5
+ 6 4 □
───────
  □ 8 2
```

(d)
```
  □ 7 7
+ 6 7 8
───────
  □ 3 5 □
```

(e)
```
  8 □ 8
+ 2 7 5
───────
  □ □ 2 3
```

(f)
```
  5 3 5 □
+ 6 9 □ 4
─────────
  □ □ 3 2 6
```

(g)
```
  □ 8 9
- 6 7 8
───────
  2 1 □
```

(h)
```
  5 2 4
- 1 5 8
───────
  □ □ □
```

(i)
```
  1 2 6 5
-   6 4 □
─────────
    □ 1 9
```

(j)
```
  □ 3 5
- 5 □ 9
───────
  1 1 □
```

(k)
```
  5 □ 4 5
- 1 8 3 □
─────────
  □ 1 □ 7
```

(l)
```
  9 0 5 2
- 6 4 □ 4
─────────
  □ □ 2 □
```

B

Solve these using a column method. Approximate first.

(a)
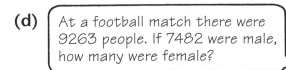
I worked 268 days last year and 278 days this year. How many days did I work in total?

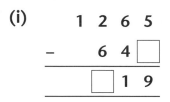

Less than 600   268
              + 278

(b)
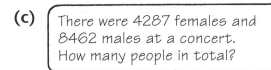
I worked 278 days last year (365 days). How many days did I not work?

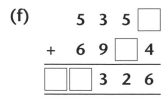

(c)

There were 4287 females and 8462 males at a concert. How many people in total?

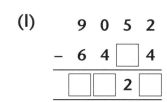

(d)
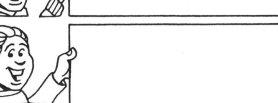
At a football match there were 9263 people. If 7482 were male, how many were female?

In part A, check each of your answers using the **inverse** operation (use subtraction to check addition, and vice versa).

Developing Numeracy
Calculations
Year 7
© A & C BLACK

Line 'em up

4769   45 143   266   7649   33 681   976   5784

1. Try to make the targets below by adding any three of the numbers above. Use approximation to help you.

Show your workings on a separate piece of paper, like this.

```
  4769
 45143
+  976
_____
 50888
  1111
```

(a)  7026

5784 + 266 + 976

(b)  39 426

(c)  10 819

(d)  53 058

(e) 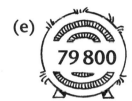 79 800

(f)  86 473

2. Make these targets by finding the difference between two of the numbers. Use approximation to help you.

(a)  1865

(b)  4808

(c)  28 912

NOW TRY THIS!

The letters A, B and C stand for different digits.

● Find what A, B and C could stand for to make all these calculations true.

```
  A B B        A C A        C C A
-   A A      + C A C      -   B B
_____      _____      _____
  A C C        B B B        A C C
```

A =
B =
C =

Remember to arrange the digits in line so that units line up with units, tens with tens, and so on. For the 'Now try this!' challenge, the letters stand for the same digits in each calculation, so make sure that the digits work for all three calculations.

Developing Numeracy Calculations Year 7 © A & C BLACK

Decimal dilemmas

A Answer these additions using a column method.

Approximate first and
show your workings. **!**

(a) 43.9 + 6.34   43.90
(About 50) +   6.34

(b) 15.58 + 9.02

(c) 134.7 + 46.43

(d) 14.63 + 235.8

(e) 465.34 + 6.8

(f) 27.95 + 92.5

B Write the missing digits in these decimal additions and subtractions.

(a)
```
   □ 3 . 6
+  5 1 . 7
───────────
   8 5 . □
```

(b)
```
   5 . □ 9
+  1 . 8 5
───────────
   □ . 0 4
```

(c)
```
   2 . 4 4
+  6 . 7 □
───────────
   □ . 2 2
```

(d)
```
   □ . 7 4
+  6 . 0 9
───────────
   □ 3 . 8 □
```

(e)
```
   3 . □ 0
+  2 . 7 5
───────────
   □ . 2 5
```

(f)
```
   3 . 5 □
+ 6 9 . □ 0
───────────
   □ 3 . 2 6
```

(g)
```
   □ . 8 9
-  6 . 7 3
───────────
   2 . 1 □
```

(h)
```
   5 . 0 6
-  1 . 5 3
───────────
   □ . □ □
```

(i)
```
  1 5 . 6 8
-    6 . 4 0
───────────
   □ . □ 8
```

(j)
```
   □ . 8 4
-  5 . □ 9
───────────
   2 . 1 □
```

(k)
```
   5 □ . 4 5
-  1 8 . 3 □
───────────
   □ 1 . □ 5
```

(l)
```
  9 0 . 7 0
- 6 4 . □ 5
───────────
  □ □ . 2 □
```

When you are adding decimals with different numbers of digits, remember
to line up the decimal points. It is sometimes helpful to write extra zeros at
the end of a decimal (for example, write 4.3 as 4.30), so that all the
decimals have the same number of digits after the decimal point.

Developing Numeracy
Calculations
Year 7
© A & C BLACK

Decimal dilemmas

C

1. (a) Choose any two of these numbers and add them together. Show your working.

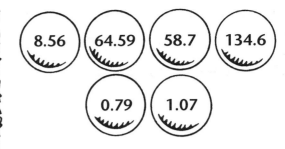

8.56	64.59	58.7	134.6
	0.79	1.07	

$$8.56$$
$$+\ 134.6$$

(b) Find your answer in the grid and colour it.

199.19	1.86	193.3	67.26
135.67	73.15	65.66	59.49
123.29	59.77	135.39	143.16
9.63	135.58	65.38	9.35

(c) Continue adding pairs of numbers. Which number in the grid cannot be made? _____

2. Make the numbers in the goldfish bowls by finding the difference between two of the numbers at the top of the page. Write the subtractions.

(a) 50.14

(b) 70.01

(c) 63.8

_____

_____

_____

NOW TRY THIS!

● Complete this magic square so that each row, column and diagonal has the total 73.05.

24.15		24.95
43.3	24.35	
	24.75	

When you are adding decimals with different numbers of digits, remember to line up the decimal points. It is sometimes helpful to write extra zeros at the end of a decimal (for example, write 4.3 as 4.30), so that all the decimals have the same number of digits after the decimal point.

Multiple methods

Look at these two different ways to solve the multiplication question.

342 × 24

	300	40	2	
20	6000	800	40	= 6840
4	1200	160	8	+ 1368
				8208

```
    3 4 2
  ×   2 4
    6 8 4 0   342 × 20
+ 1 3 6 8     342 × 4
    8 2 0 8
```

1. Solve these questions using the first method (the grid method).

(a) 23 × 325

(b) 35 × 144

(c) 56 × 462

(d) 26 × 353

2. Solve these questions using the second method.

(a)
```
    2 3 1
  ×   3 6
          231 x 30
+ _____   231 x 6
```

(b)
```
    4 2 9
  ×   5 3
+ _____
```

(c)
```
    3 8 5
  ×   4 7
+ _____
```

3. Which of the two methods did you find easier? _____

Why? _____

Do these multiplications on another piece of paper. Tick the correct answer.

(a) 342 × 27	9384	☐	9234	☐	9514	☐	9334	☐
(b) 258 × 33	8514	☐	8504	☐	8414	☐	6504	☐
(c) 146 × 49	7244	☐	7054	☐	7264	☐	7154	☐
(d) 294 × 36	9584	☐	10 484	☐	10 584	☐	9574	☐
(e) 518 × 58	30 044	☐	29 944	☐	30 034	☐	29 844	☐

For part B, choose whichever method you find easier. (Do not use a calculator.) Remember how to multiply a number by a multiple of 10: for example, for 5 × 40, you can think of 5 × 4 = 20 and then make this answer ten times larger.

**Developing Numeracy
Calculations
Year 7
© A & C BLACK**

Multiple methods

C

1. Use a written method of multiplication to find the number of each item on the list. Make approximations first. Show your workings on the back of this sheet.

Item	Number of tins per box	Number of boxes	Approximate number of tins	Exact number of tins
Baked beans	24	137		
Sweetcorn	12	263		
Ravioli	42	274		
Spaghetti	48	426		
Meatballs	16	853		
Carrots	28	336		
Mushrooms	36	587		
Tuna	56	658		

2. Check your answers **without** using the ☒ key.

Write what you key in to check your first answer. _____

NOW TRY THIS!

A three-digit number and a two-digit number have been made with the digits 1, 2, 3, 4 and 5. The two numbers are multiplied together to get the answer 5940.

● What are the two numbers?

☐☐☐ × ☐☐ = 5940

When you are multiplying large numbers, always make sure you have an approximate idea of how large the answer will be. Remember how to multiply a number by a multiple of 10: for example, for 5 × 40, you can think of 5 × 4 = 20 and then make this answer ten times larger.

Crack it!

A

Use your knowledge of tables facts to help you answer these questions.

For 0.4 × 5, think of 4 × 5 = 20. Then make this answer ten times smaller (as 0.4 is ten times smaller than 4).

(a) 0.4 × 5 = ___2___   **(b)** 0.02 × 8 = _____   **(c)** 0.3 × 6 = _____

(d) 0.7 × 4 = _____   **(e)** 0.04 × 6 = _____   **(f)** 0.03 × 9 = _____

(g) 0.08 × 3 = _____   **(h)** 0.9 × 7 = _____   **(i)** 0.9 × 9 = _____

(j) 0.7 × 6 = _____   **(k)** 0.05 × 7 = _____   **(l)** 0.08 × 7 = _____

B

Look at these two different ways to solve the multiplication question.

	8	0.4	0.03
5	40	2	0.15

= 42.15

8.43 × 5

```
  8 . 4 3
×       5
4 2 . 1 5
    2   1
```
Approximate first:
(about 8 × 5 = 40)

1. Solve these questions using the first method (the grid method).

(a) 6.35 × 4

(b) 3.48 × 6

(c) 8.55 × 7

(d) 3.59 × 8

2. Solve these questions using the second method. Make an approximation first.

(a) 4 . 3 6 (about _____)
         ×   5
         _____

(b) 7 . 5 9 (about _____)
         ×   8
         _____

(c) 5 . 5 8 (about _____)
         ×   6
         _____

(d) 1 2 . 0 6 (about _____)
         ×   7
         _____

3. Which of the two methods did you find easier? _____

Why? _____

 Remember that when you make a number ten times smaller, all the digits move one place to the right and the decimal point stays in the same place (for example, 15 ÷ 10 = 1.5 and 4.7 ÷ 10 = 0.47).

Developing Numeracy
Calculations
Year 7
© A & C BLACK

Crack it!

C

1. Use a written method to answer these questions. Find each answer in the code below and circle its corresponding letter.

(a) A mug costs £3.78. How much do seven mugs cost ?	
(b) Mr Mann gives £6.47 to each of his four children. How much does he give away?	
(c) A sofa is 1.68 m long. A shop wants to display six sofas in a line. How much space will it need?	
(d) A bag of apples weighs 2.55 kg. How much do nine bags weigh?	
(e) A CD costs £14.39. How much do eight CDs cost?	
(f) Seven houses are joined as a terrace. Each house is 3.92 m wide. Find the width of the terrace.	
(g) One ticket costs £25.36. How much do six tickets cost?	"FUNKY MONKEY" IN CONCERT £25.36
(h) Four suitcases each weigh 19.71 kg. What is the total mass of the four cases?	
(i) I think of a number and divide it by 6. The answer is 13.84. What is my number?	
(j) I think of a number and divide it by 9. The answer is 16.08. What is my number?	

Workings

E	X	U	B	L	N	A	T	E	Q	I	V
115.12	42.22	152.16	25.59	144.72	22.95	83.04	78.84	10.08	25.88	26.46	27.44

2. Rearrange the circled letters to make a mathematical word. _____

NOW TRY THIS!

● Complete these multiplications using the cards. Use each card once only in each calculation. | 1 | 2 | 3 | 4 | · |

(a) ☐☐☐ × ☐ = 4.92   **(b)** ☐☐☐ × ☐ = 8.62

(c) ☐☐☐ × ☐ = 128.4   **(d)** ☐☐☐ × ☐ = 42.6

When you are multiplying decimals, always remember to make an approximation first to help you be sure that your answer is about the right size.

**Developing Numeracy
Calculations
Year 7**
© A & C BLACK

45

Share and share alike

A 1.  Solve these division questions. Use the method shown, or one of your own. Approximate first.

All the answers are whole numbers. **!**

(a) 595 ÷ 35

About _20_

```
35)595
  − 350    35 x 10
    245
  − 140    35 x 4
    105
  −  70    35 x 2
     35
  −  35    35 x 1
```
Answer: 17

(b) 338 ÷ 26

About _____

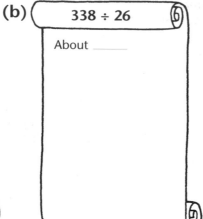

(c) 943 ÷ 41

About _____

(d) 756 ÷ 27

About _____

(e) 722 ÷ 19

About _____

(f) 858 ÷ 33

About _____

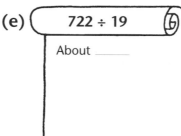

2. Check your answers **without** using the ÷ key.

Write what you key in to check your first answer. _____

B Find and correct the error in each calculation.

(a) 943 ÷ 23

```
23)943
  − 460    23 × 20
    483
  − 460    23 × 20
     23
  −  23    23 × 1
      0
```
Answer: **23**

(b) 468 ÷ 26

```
26)468
  − 260    26 × 10
    208
  − 130    26 × 5
     78
  −  26    26 × 1
     52
```
Answer: **16 r 52**

(c) 816 ÷ 34

```
34)816
  − 340    34 × 10
    536
  − 340    34 × 10
    196
  − 170    34 × 5
     26
```
Answer: **25 r 26**

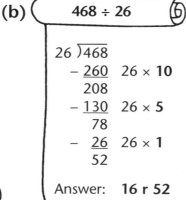

To check your answers to division questions, multiply your answer by the second number in the division question (for example, to check 74.4 ÷ 6 = 12.4, do 12.4 x 6 to see whether it equals 74.4).

Share and share alike

C

Read the instructions carefully.

☆ Choose a three-digit number and a two-digit number from these cards.

☆ Divide the larger number by the smaller one. Use a written method and show your working. (Remember to approximate first.)

| 408 |
| 578 |
| 782 |
| 986 |

÷

| 34 |
| 68 |
| 85 |

Follow the instructions to find divisions which give these answers.

(a) 23

(b) 6

(c) 29

(d) 8.5 (or $8\frac{1}{2}$)

(e) 6.8 (or 6 r 68)

(f) 11.6 (or 11 r 33)

Workings

NOW TRY THIS!

● Solve these problems using a written method. Circle the answer closest to £42.50.

(a)

18 people share a lottery win of £756. How much do they each win?

£

(b)
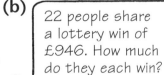

22 people share a lottery win of £946. How much do they each win?

£

(c)

15 people share a lottery win of £633. How much do they each win?

£

To check your answers to division questions, multiply your answer by the second number in the division question (for example, to check 74.4 ÷ 6 = 12.4, do 12.4 × 6 to see whether it equals 74.4).

Divide and rule!

A 1. 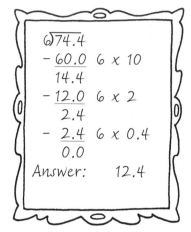 Find the answers using the method shown, or one of your own. Approximate first.

(a) $74.4 \div 6$

About _12.5_

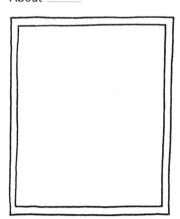

```
6)74.4
 - 60.0   6 x 10
   14.4
 - 12.0   6 x 2
    2.4
 -  2.4   6 x 0.4
    0.0
Answer:    12.4
```

(b) $58.8 \div 7$

About _____

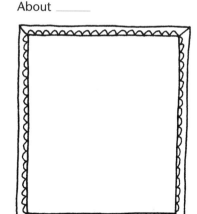

(c) $78.4 \div 8$

About _____

(d) $21.4 \div 5$

About _____

(e) $106.8 \div 8$

About _____

(f) $45.78 \div 7$

About _____

2. Check your answers **without** using the ÷ key.

Write what you key in to check your first answer. _____

B All the rows, columns and diagonals in this magic square add up to the same number.

Create a second magic square by dividing each number in the first square by 4.

Do all the rows, columns and diagonals add up to the same number?

÷ 4

110.08	84.96	210.56
235.68	135.2	34.72
59.84	185.44	160.32

27.52		

 To check your answers to division questions, multiply your answer by the second number in the division question (for example, to check $74.4 \div 6 = 12.4$, do 12.4×6 to see whether it equals 74.4).

Developing Numeracy
Calculations
Year 7
© A & C BLACK

Divide and rule!

C

1. Solve the division problems using a written method. Shade the correct answer.

(a) Four tickets for a West End show cost £95.84. What is the cost of one ticket?

£21.96   £23.96   £91.84

(b) Eight CDs cost a total of £78.32. What is the mean cost of each CD?

£8.97   £7.98   £9.79

(c) Seven friends go to a restaurant. The bill is £107.24. If they split the bill equally, how much will each pay?

£13.32   £14.32   £15.32

(d) At Sports Day, Jan throws the javelin a total of 289.6 m in eight throws. What is her average throw?

26.2 m   281.6 m   36.2 m

(e) Five sisters buy identical T-shirts. The total cost is £44.45. What is the price of a T-shirt?

£7.89   £8.89   £9.89

(f) Mark and Kylie walk a total of 108.32 km during an eight-day hike. What is their mean daily distance?

13.54 km   14.54 km   15.54 km

(g) Two engineers lay 111.24 m of cable. It takes nine hours. How many metres do they lay per hour on average?

13.36 m   6.18 m   12.36 m

(h) I think of a number. When I multiply it by 7 the answer is 111.09. What is my number?

16.48   777.63   15.87

2. Discuss your division method and answers with a partner.

NOW TRY THIS!

● Answer these questions using a written method. Circle the odd one out.

(a) $237.76 \div 8$

(b) $118.56 \div 4$

(c) $177.84 \div 6$

Remember that you can find the **mean** average by dividing the total by the number of items (for example, the total amount spent by the number of items bought).

Canny keys

A

1. Answer these questions. To enter negative numbers, use the sign change key, which looks like this: (–) or +/–.

Remember to check your answers.

(a) 423 – 296   = _____   **(b)** 357 – 461   = _____   **(c)** 406 – 712   = _____

(d) 507 – 689   = _____   **(e)** 210 – 599   = _____   **(f)** 492 – 800   = _____

(g) 782 – 1093   = _____   **(h)** 2987 – 3482   = _____   **(i)** ⁻142 + 176   = _____

(j) ⁻351 + 128   = _____   **(k)** ⁻385 + 294   = _____   **(l)** ⁻830 + 573   = _____

(m) ⁻1056 + 997 = _____   **(n)** ⁻2803 + 2799 = _____   **(o)** 75 + ⁻56   = _____

(p) 123 + ⁻157   = _____   **(q)** 351 + ⁻412   = _____   **(r)** 399 + ⁻400   = _____

(s) 121 – ⁻121   = _____   **(t)** 156 – ⁻44   = _____   **(u)** 389 – ⁻111   = _____

2. Use the squaring key x^2 and the square root key $\sqrt{}$ to answer these questions.

(a) 15^2 = _____   **(b)** 19^2 = _____   **(c)** 27^2 = _____

(d) 46^2 = _____   **(e)** 77^2 = _____   **(f)** 99^2 = _____

(g) $\sqrt{529}$ = _____   **(h)** $\sqrt{961}$ = _____   **(i)** $\sqrt{2916}$ = _____

(j) $\sqrt{4225}$ = _____   **(k)** $\sqrt{5329}$ = _____   **(l)** $\sqrt{9604}$ = _____

B

Use the brackets keys ( ) to answer these questions.

(a) (6 + 3) × 4 – 10 × (6 + 1) = _____   **(b)** 6 + (3 × 4) – 10 × (6 + 1) = _____

(c) (6 + 3) × 4 – (10 × 6) + 1 = _____   **(d)** 6 + (3 × 4) – (10 × 6) + 1 = _____

(e) (6 + 3) × (4 – 10) × 6 + 1 = _____   **(f)** 6 + 3 × (4 – 10) × (6 + 1) = _____

Make sure you know which is the **sign change** key on your calculator. On some calculators it shows +/– and on others it shows (–). Ask your teacher if you are not sure. For part B, if your calculator does not have brackets keys you will need to work out the part of the calculation in brackets first.

Developing Numeracy
Calculations
Year 7
© A & C BLACK

Canny keys

To answer this calculation, key in (8.4 − 3.6) ÷ (8.4 + 3.6). The answer is 0.4.

1. Use this method to answer the questions.

(a) $\dfrac{5.6 + 8.2}{5.6 - 8.2}$ = _____

(b) $\dfrac{13.2 - 6.1}{13.2 + 6.1}$ = _____

(c) $\dfrac{7.6 - 5.7}{7.6 + 5.7}$ = _____

(d) $\dfrac{4.2 + 5.8}{4.2 - 5.8}$ = _____

(e) $\dfrac{12.1 + 9.2}{2.3 + 3.7}$ = _____

(f) $\dfrac{4.6 \times 5.3}{5.4 - 2.1}$ = _____

(g) $\dfrac{4.2 + 15.6}{16.3 \div 4.7}$ = _____

(h) $\dfrac{8.4 \times 5.1}{4.3 \times 5.7}$ = _____

(i) $\dfrac{17.1 + 11.3}{2.4 \times 2.4}$ = _____

(j) $\dfrac{15.6 \div 4}{12 \div 3}$ = _____

(k) $\dfrac{24.6 \div 8.2}{26.4 \div 2.8}$ = _____

(l) $\dfrac{8.8 \times 8.8}{8.8 \div 8.8}$ = _____

2. Choose pairs of cards and arrange them as shown. What different answers can you make?

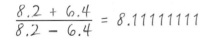

| 8.2 | 3.6 | 4.8 | 6.4 | 7.6 |

☐ + ☐
―――――
☐ − ☐

! Use the same two numbers on the top and bottom.

$\dfrac{8.2 + 6.4}{8.2 - 6.4}$ = 8.11111111

NOW TRY THIS!

- Key each of these into your calculator and write the answers.

(a) 38^2 _____   **(b)** $(^-38)^2$ _____   **(c)** 57^2 _____   **(d)** $(^-57)^2$ _____

- What do you notice? _____
- Write two more pairs of numbers which have the same square. _____

Think about it!

When you are using a calculator, think carefully about the number shown on the display.

Is it a time question?

Do I need to round?

Do I need to write the answer differently?

Is the question about money?

1. Answer these questions using a calculator and write a sensible answer for each.

(a) £5.84 × 40 = ~~233.6~~ £233.60   **(b)** £1.08 × 90 = _____

(c) £17 ÷ 5   = _____   **(d)** £1.62 ÷ 18 = _____

(e) £384 ÷ 24 = _____   **(f)** 27p × 90 = _____

(g) 59p × 14 = _____   **(h)** £51 ÷ 68 = _____

(i) £36 ÷ 90 = _____   **(j)** £11 ÷ 3   = _____

(k) £10 ÷ 9   = _____   **(l)** £7 ÷ 6   = _____

2. Use a calculator and give your answers in hours and minutes.

(a) 6 hours ÷ 4   = _1 hr 30 min_

(b) 5 hours ÷ 4   = _____

(c) 7 hours ÷ 4   = _____   **(d)** 7 hours 30 min ÷ 2 = _____

(e) 9 hours 45 min ÷ 3 = _____   **(f)** 9 hours ÷ 6   = _____

(g) 2 hours 15 min × 6 = _____   **(h)** 1 hour 45 min × 5 = _____

> **!** Remember: half an hour (0.5) is 30 minutes, one-quarter (0.25) is 15 minutes and three-quarters (0.75) is 45 minutes.

Use this diagram and a calculator to convert the measurements.

years	days	hours	minutes	seconds

× 365   × 24   × 60   × 60

(a) 5 years = _____ days   **(b)** 17 hours = _____ minutes

(c) 7 days = _____ hours   **(d)** 16 minutes = _____ seconds

(e) 2 days = _____ minutes   **(f)** 3 hours = _____ seconds

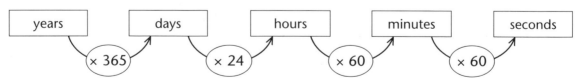

When you are using a calculator, it is a good idea to get into the habit of placing it on the table and keying in with your non-writing hand. This will leave your writing hand free to record answers. It may feel strange at first, but will save you lots of time later.

Developing Numeracy
Calculations
Year 7
© A & C BLACK

Think about it!

The calculator display interpret

1. Read this question carefully.

Sanjay has £477. He buys as many CDs as he can with his money. They cost £13 each. How much money does he have left over?

(a) Jo used a calculator to answer the question and got the answer 36.692307. This is **not** the correct answer. Can you say why?

_____

(b) How many CDs can Sanjay buy? _____

(c) Work out how much money Sanjay has left over. Show your working and talk to a partner about your method.

Working

2. Answer these questions.

(a) Chloe has £178. She buys as many CDs as she can with her money. They cost **£13** each. How much money does she have left over? _____

(b) David has £346. He buys as many CDs as he can with his money. They cost **£13** each. How much money does he have left over? _____

(c) Bella has £229. She buys as many CDs as she can with her money. They cost **£18** each. How much money does she have left over? _____

NOW TRY THIS!

● Convert these hours into days and hours.

Divide by 24 and then find the number of hours left over.

(a) 475 hours is the same as _____ days and _____ hours.

(b) 950 hours is the same as _____ days and _____ hours.

When you are using a calculator, it is a good idea to get into the habit of placing it on the table and keying in with your non-writing hand. This will leave your writing hand free to record answers. It may feel strange at first, but will save you lots of time later.

Developing Numeracy Calculations Year 7 © A & C BLACK 53

Let's investigate

A

Here are three ⬚ consecutive ⬚ numbers. Harry has noticed a pattern in the numbers using his calculator.

| 29 | 30 | 31 |

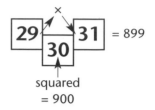 = 899

If I multiply **29** and **31**, I get 899.
If I key in **30²** I get 900.
900 is one more than 899.

squared
= 900

1. Write sets of consecutive numbers in the boxes and test Harry's pattern.

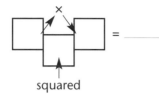 = _____

squared

= _____

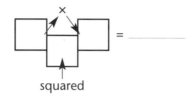 = _____

squared

= _____

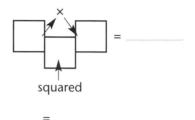 = _____

squared

= _____

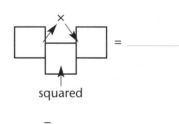 = _____

squared

= _____

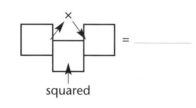 = _____

squared

= _____

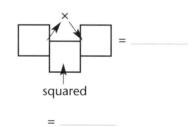 = _____

squared

= _____

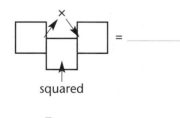 = _____

squared

= _____

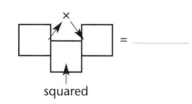 = _____

squared

= _____

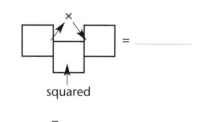 = _____

squared

= _____

2. Do you think Harry's pattern works for all consecutive numbers? _____

Explain your thinking. _____

_____

B

Investigate which number you would multiply **38** by to get these answers:

(a) 3838 _____   **(b)** 383 838 _____

(c) ⁻38 _____

  Consecutive numbers are numbers that come one after another in order (for example, 5, 6, 7 or 17, 18, 19, 20, 21). **Squaring** a number means multiplying the number by itself. When you use a calculator to square a number, multiply the number by itself or use the x^2 key.

Developing Numeracy
Calculations
Year 7
© A & C BLACK

C Harry has noticed a pattern in these five **consecutive** numbers using his calculator.

| 28 | 29 | 30 | 31 | 32 |

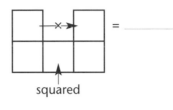

If I multiply **28** and **32**, I get 896.
If I key in **30²** I get 900.
900 is four more than 896.

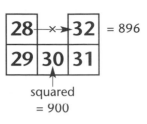

28 —×→ 32 = 896

29 30 31

squared = 900

1. Write sets of consecutive numbers in the boxes and test Harry's pattern.

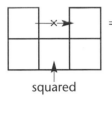

squared

= _____

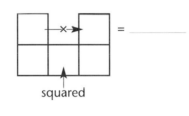

squared

= _____

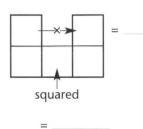

squared

= _____

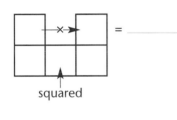

squared

= _____

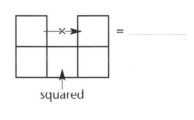

squared

= _____

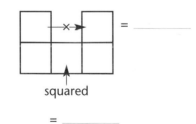

squared

= _____

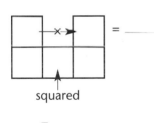

squared

= _____

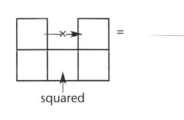

squared

= _____

squared

= _____

2. Do you think Harry's pattern works for all consecutive numbers? _____

Explain your thinking. _____

_____

NOW TRY THIS!

An adult's ticket costs three times as much as a child's ticket.

● What is the price of an adult's ticket if two adults' and two children's tickets cost £14.80? _____

● Write another ticket price puzzle for a partner to solve.

Consecutive numbers are numbers that come one after another in order (for example, 5, 6, 7 or 17, 18, 19, 20, 21). **Squaring** a number means multiplying the number by itself. When you use a calculator to square a number, multiply the number by itself or use the x^2 key.

Developing Numeracy
Calculations
Year 7
© A & C BLACK

55

Check it out!

A Complete the rows to show the rules for adding and subtracting odd and even numbers.

	Question	Example	Answer
(a)	Odd + Odd	365 + 693	*Even*
(b)	Odd + Even	667 + 978	
(c)		536 + 224	
(d)	Even + Odd		
(e)	Odd – Odd	365 – 693	
(f)		1585 – 842	
(g)		3360 – 694	
(h)	Even – Odd		
(i)	Odd + Odd + Odd	365 + 693 + 593	
(j)	Odd + Even + Odd	365 + 698 + 593	
(k)	Even + Even + Odd		
(l)		644 + 768 + 930	
(m)		930 + 767 + _____	Odd

B **Without** doing the whole calculation, write the last digit (units digit) of the answer.

(a) 23 × 125   5

(b) 428 × 217

(c) 647 × 246

(d) 548 × 481

(e) 424 × 649

(f) 814 × 758

(g) 739 × 912

(h) 965 × 175

(i) 813 × 388

(j) 490 × 723

(k) 399 × 143

(l) 909 × 470

(m) 589 × 311

(n) 437 × 217

(o) 444 × 643

 If you add an odd number and an even number together and you get an even answer, you know that your answer must be wrong! In part B, multiply the last digit of each number together to find the last digit of the answer. You can use this as a checking method.

Developing Numeracy
Calculations
Year 7
© A & C BLACK

56

Check it out!

C 1. Check these answers by following the instructions in the boxes.
Do **not** work out the exact answers.

> Look at the units digit of these answers.
> Put a cross next to any that are incorrect.

(a) 348 + 498 = 845   **(b)** 275 + 452 = 727

(c) 367 – 465 = ⁻98   **(d)** 285 – 148 = 136

(e) 48 × 49 = 2352   **(f)** 275 × 452 = 124 752

> Find an approximate answer to these questions by rounding.
> Put a cross next to any that are incorrect.

(g) 348 + 498 = 846   **(h)** 789 + 408 = 119.7

(i) 496 – 329 – 167   **(j)** 759 – 126 – 433

(k) 19 × 49 = 631   **(l)** 106 × 389 = 41 234

> Look at the last digit of these answers **and** find an approximate
> answer by rounding. Put a cross next to any that are incorrect.

(m) 259 + 975 = 1235   **(n)** 5846 + 452 = 6298

(o) 6548 – 1367 = 811   **(p)** 2976 – 1238 = 1738

(q) 18 × 99 = 1781   **(r)** 29 × 91 = 1639

2.  Now use a calculator to check all the answers, using the **inverse** operation.

Write what you key in to check the first answer. _____

NOW TRY THIS!

- Work out approximate answers to these questions, by rounding.

(a) 31.7 × 5.9 = _____   **(b)** 1.9 × 19.95 = _____

(c) 20.7 × 4.91 = _____   **(d)** 10.18 × 0.98 = _____

(e) 39.7 × 3.04 = _____   **(f)** 48.78 × 7.89 = _____

 To work out approximate answers, round the numbers in the question
to the nearest whole number, ten, hundred or thousand. Then do the
calculation using the rounded numbers. Remember that the **inverse** of
addition is subtraction, and the **inverse** of multiplication is division.

What's wrong?

A

Write an explanation to show what mistake each person has made.

(a)

How many lots of 6 are there in 75?

I key in 6 ÷ 75 on my calculator and get 0.08. There are 0.08 lots of 6 in 75.

(b)

What is the cost of eight cans costing 48p each?

I key in 48 x 8 on my calculator and get 384. The cost is £384.

(c)

What is the sum of £3.57 and 65p?

I key in 3.57 + 65 and get 68.57. The sum of the two amounts is £68.57.

(d)

How many 26p stamps can you buy for £5?

I key in 26 ÷ 5 and get 5.2. This means I can get five stamps.

B

Use a calculator to find the correct answer for each question above. Show how you worked out the answers and how you checked them.

(a)	(b)
(c)	(d)

To check your answers you could use the **inverse** operation: for example, use subtraction to check addition and use multiplication to check division (and vice versa).

Developing Numeracy
Calculations
Year 7
© A & C BLACK

What's wrong?

C Play this game with a partner. You each need a copy of this sheet, paper and a calculator.

☆ Each choose two numbers from the grid and write them on another piece of paper in an addition, subtraction, multiplication or division question.

☆ Use a calculator to find the answer to your question, but keep it a secret.

☆ Write your question on this sheet under 'My questions', and write three possible answers (one of them must be the correct one).

☆ Swap sheets with your partner. Tick the answer you think is correct. Do **not** use a calculator. Score 1 point if you have chosen the correct answer.

☆ Repeat seven times. The winner is the player with the most points at the end.

3	467	785	5	63	966	2
820	584	693	655	13	86	36
790	111	42	292	56	999	23

My questions	My possible answers	My partner's score

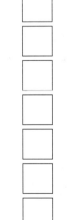

● Use **inverse** operations to solve these missing number questions. Start with the answer and work back through the question. Check your answers carefully.

(a) (☐ − 5) × 2 = 16   **(b)** (☐ + 7) ÷ 5 = 4   **(c)** (☐ × 2) ÷ 8 + 1 = 5

16 ÷ 2 + 5 =

When you are choosing from your partner's possible answers in part C, use checking strategies to help you work out an approximate answer (for example, look at the last digit of the answer, or use rounding). Remember that the **inverse** of addition is subtraction, and the **inverse** of multiplication is division.

Answers

p 8

A1 Example answers:

(a) 482 + 482
(b) 167 + 167 + 167
(c) 7480 ÷ 2
(d) 5680 + 6
(e) 2390 + 239
(f) 4310 + 431
(g) 9410 − 941
(h) 1034 ÷ 22
(i) 4176 ÷ 58
(j) 2448 ÷ 72
(k) 1411 ÷ 83
(l) 15 600 + 156
(m) 34 200 − 342

B
(a) 0   1   0
(b) 1   0   0
(c) 58   0   1
(d) 0   1   0

p 9

C1 Example answers:

(a) 243 − 81 − 81 − 81
(b) 237 − 79 − 79 − 79
(c) 204 − 68 − 68 − 68
(d) 292 − 73 − 73 − 73 − 73
(e) 376 − 94 − 94 − 94 − 94
(f) 18 × 43
(g) 29 × 85
(h) 58 × 72
(i) 96 × 129

p 10

A
(a) 8 r 4
(b) £8.50
(c) 9
(d) 8.5 or $8\frac{1}{2}$
(e) 8.5 or $8\frac{1}{2}$
(f) 8
(g) 9
(h) £8.50
(i) 9
(j) 8.5 or $8\frac{1}{2}$

p 11

C1
(a) 33.925714
    33
(b) 28.378378
    29
(c) 11.9825
    £11.98
(d) 8.0909091
    8
(e) 1.1916666
    £1.19
(f) 10.434782
    10
(g) 17.333333
    17
(h) 82.1875
    82 000 g

Now try this!
(a) True   (b) False (a number divided by 0 gives infinity)
(c) True   (d) False (4 divided by $\frac{1}{2}$ = 8)
(e) False (8 divided by $-\frac{1}{2}$ = ⁻8)

p 12

A1
(a) 140   (b) 130
(c) 480   (d) 180
(e) 160   (f) 180
(g) 360   (h) 630
(i) 270   (j) 1500
(k) 130   (l) 180

A2
(a) 30   (b) 30
(c) 240   (d) 240
(e) 60   (f) 60
(g) 36   (h) 36

B
(a) (8 × 2) + 4   (b) 8 + (4 × 2)
(c) (8 × 4) + 2   (d) 2 × (8 + 4)
(e) (8 + 2) × 4   (f) (4 + 2) × 8

p 13

C1
(a) ✓   ✓   ✓
     ×   ✓   ×
     ✓   ✓   ✓
     ✓   ✓   ✓

C2
(a) 51.7   (b) 40.3
(c) 272.7   (d) 425.7
(e) 554.4   (f) 92.4
(g) 686.8   (h) 431.2

Now try this!
Both statements are true.

p 14

A
(a) + 36 =   (b) × 54 =
(c) − 79 =   (d) + 47 =
(e) ÷ 34 =   (f) × 62 =
(g) ÷ 0.42 =   (h) × 4 =
(i) × 5 ÷ 3 =   (j) × 7 ÷ 5 =

B
(a) correct 13
(b) incorrect 6 × 4.25 = 25.5
(c) incorrect 168 ÷ 8 = 21
(d) incorrect 418 + 875 = 1293
(e) correct 29.38 − 4.8 = 24.58
(f) incorrect 40.65 ÷ 5 = 8.13
(g) correct 0.095 × 6 = 0.57

p 15

C1
(a) 5 8 14 23 26 29 62 65 92
(b) +6 ⟵ ÷3 ⟵ −2

C2
(a) 36 41 51 66 71 76 131 136 181
    −2 ⟵ ÷5 ⟵ +9
(b) 17 19 23 29 31 33 55 57 75
    ÷4 ⟵ −6 ⟵ ×2

Now try this!
(a) 10
(b) 34
(c) 6

p 16

A2

(a)
0.1^2	=	0.1	×	0.1	=	0.01
0.2^2	=	0.2	×	0.2	=	0.02
0.3^2	=	0.3	×	0.3	=	0.09
0.4^2	=	0.4	×	0.4	=	0.16
0.5^2	=	0.5	×	0.5	=	0.25
0.6^2	=	0.6	×	0.6	=	0.36

(b)
0.7^2	=	0.7	×	0.7	=	0.49
0.8^2	=	0.8	×	0.8	=	0.64
0.9^2	=	0.9	×	0.9	=	0.81
1.0^2	=	1.0	×	1.0	=	1.0
1.1^2	=	1.1	×	1.1	=	1.21
1.2^2	=	1.2	×	1.2	=	1.44

B
- $\sqrt{8100} \longrightarrow 90$
- $\sqrt{49} \longrightarrow 7$
- $\sqrt{6400} \longrightarrow 80$
- $\sqrt{36} \longrightarrow 6$
- $\sqrt{0.25} \longrightarrow 0.5$
- $\sqrt{0.04} \longrightarrow 0.2$
- $\sqrt{0.16} \longrightarrow 0.4$
- $\sqrt{100} \longrightarrow 10$
- $\sqrt{1} \longrightarrow 1$
- $\sqrt{0.01} \longrightarrow 0.1$
- $\sqrt{3600} \longrightarrow 60$
- $\sqrt{1.44} \longrightarrow 1.2$
- $\sqrt{0.09} \longrightarrow 0.3$
- $\sqrt{1.21} \longrightarrow 1.1$

p 17

C1

¹1	0	²6		³1	2	⁴8		⁵2	
6		⁶4	0	4		⁷5	0	0	
	⁸1	0		⁹9	¹⁰7			0	
¹¹6	4		¹²1		¹³2	8	¹⁴8		
¹⁵1	5		¹⁶4	8			¹⁷4	0	
			¹⁸1	4		¹⁹2	0		
²⁰1	0	3		²¹3	6		²²1	3	
6		²³1	²⁴2		²⁵5	0	0		
²⁶9	0		²⁷3	4			²⁸9	9	

C2
- (a) 12
- (b) 40
- (c) 5
- (d) 3
- (e) 4
- (f) 1

p 18

A
(a) 13	(b) 63	(c) 26
(d) 8	(e) 15	(f) 2
(g) 12	(h) 10	(i) 3
(j) 36	(k) 10	(l) 30
(m) 19	(n) 36	(o) 15

B
(a) ✓	(b) 30	(c) ✓
(d) ✓	(e) 22	(f) ✓
(g) ✓	(h) 1	(i) 1
(j) ✓	(k) ✓	(l) ✓
(m) 1	(n) 2	(o) $\frac{3}{4}$
(p) ✓	(q) ✓	(r) $\frac{1}{2}$
(s) ✓	(t) ✓	(u) ✓

p 19

C1
(a) 3	(b) 2
(c) 1	(d) 4
(e) 7	(f) 3
(g) 16	(h) 5
(i) 11	(j) 1
(k) 27	

C2
(a) 10	(b) 2	(c) 2
(d) 2	(e) 15	(f) 2

Now try this!
(a) 48	(b) 78	(c) 1
(d) 1	(e) 8	(f) $-\frac{9}{6} = -1\frac{1}{2}$

p 20

A1
- (a) 21
- (b) 24
- (c) C16, D18, E23

A2
- (a)
A	B	C	D	E
15	11	13	11	15
- (b)
A	B	C	D	E
30	48	66	30	42

A3
- (a) double 3.6
- (b) half 32
- (c) $8^2 + 1$
- (d) half 36
- (e) 0.2×19
- (f) $1 - 0.02$

B
- $400 \times 0.8 \longrightarrow 320$
- $0.04 \times 0.8 \longrightarrow 0.032$
- $0.4 \times 8 \longrightarrow 3.2$
- $4 \times 0.8 \longrightarrow 3.2$
- $40 \times 0.8 \longrightarrow 32$
- $0.4 \times 80 \longrightarrow 32$
- $0.4 \times 0.8 \longrightarrow 0.32$
- $4 \times 8 \longrightarrow 32$
- $0.04 \times 8 \longrightarrow 0.32$
- $4 \times 0.08 \longrightarrow 0.32$

p 21

C1
- (a) ✓
- (b) ×
- (c) ✓
- (d) ×
- (e) ✓

Now try this!
(a) 27	(b) 9	(c) 2	(d) 81
(e) 180	(f) 5	(g) 102	(h) 163

p 22

A1
(a) 400	(b) 3	(c) 1200
(d) 1.7	(e) 450	(f) 3.25
(g) 75	(h) 4	(i) 0.17

A2
÷10	÷1000	÷1000	÷1000
×10	×1000	×1000	×1000

A3
(a) 34	(b) 46.5
(c) 4.6	(d) 2840
(e) 63 000	(f) 0.46
(g) 670	(h) 5.275
(i) 6500	(j) 1.88
(k) 7284	(l) 0.034

B1
÷60	÷60	÷24	÷365

B2
(a) 3	(b) 20
(c) 2	(d) 240
(e) 48	(f) 720

p 23

C1
(a) 24 cm, 32 cm²	(b) 28 cm, 45 cm²
(c) 22 cm, 28 cm²	(d) 18 cm, 20 cm²
(e) 44 cm, 120 cm²	(f) 36 cm, 77 cm²
(g) 42 cm, 108 cm²	(h) 48 cm, 144 cm²
(i) 56 cm, 147 cm²	

C2
(a) 8 cm, 5 cm	(b) 10 cm, 5 cm	(c) 13 cm, 1 cm

Now try this!
- (a) $a = 18 \text{ cm}^2$ $b = 9 \text{ cm}^2$ c and d = 4.5 cm²
- (b) $a = 50 \text{ cm}^2$ $b = 25 \text{ cm}^2$ c and d = 12.5 cm²
- (c) $a = 24.5 \text{ cm}^2$ $b = 12.25 \text{ cm}^2$ c and d = 6.125 cm²

p 24

A1
94	68	172	194	154	84	146	57
136	15.2	7.2	7.6	13.8	8.6	5.9	19

A2
(a) 95	(b) 147
(c) 135	(d) 171

B (a) 15.7 (b) 17.3
(c) 13.5 (d) 19.1
(e) 11.7 (f) 15.3

p 25
C1 (a) 4.7
(b) 5.5
(c) 9.7
(d) 4.3
(e) 7.9
C2 (a) £8.80 (b) 4.8
(c) 64p (d) £73.50
(e) £8.60 (f) 86p
(g) £1001 (h) £1.92

Now try this!
(a) 814
(b) 613
(c) 1299

p 26
A (a) 725 (b) 951
(c) 563 (d) 753
(e) 1122 (f) 839
B (a) 155 (b) 169
(c) 189 (d) 201
(e) 659 (f) 177

p 27
C1 (a) 7.6 (b) 9.6
(c) 15.4 (d) 4.5
(e) 8.8 (f) 3.37
C2 (a) 8.4 (b) 12.6 (c) 15.5
(d) 15.2 (e) 21.2 (f) 39.4
(g) 13.51 (h) 14.1 (i) 14.31
(j) 1.6 (k) 2.8 (l) 5.9
(m) 11.6 (n) 13.6 (o) 33.6
(p) 3.53 (q) 3.12 (r) 4.35

Now try this!
£20.97 £41.94 £30.89
£34.93 £23.88 £44.85

p 28
B (a) 494 (b) 184 (c) 299
(d) 418 (e) 347 (f) 711
(g) 313 (h) 501 (i) 623
(j) 943 (k) 401 (l) 935

p 29
Now try this!
£1.94 £7.10 £4.08
£5.16 £3.02 £2.14

p 30
A (a) 126 (b) 70 (c) 219
(d) 128 (e) 126 (f) 159
(g) 72 (h) 168 (i) 276
B1 (a) 16 (b) 35 (c) 25
(d) 32 (e) 55 (f) 54
B2 (a) 31 (b) 71 (c) 38
(d) 64 (e) 61 (f) 58

p 31
C1 (a) 210 (b) 310 (c) 340
(d) 410 (e) 430 (f) 440
(g) 285 (h) 345 (i) 385
(j) 1200 (k) 1800 (l) 2200
(m) 3300 (n) 4200 (o) 4400
(p) 1550 (q) 1850 (r) 2750

C2 (a) 120 (b) 150 (c) 210
(d) 180 (e) 270 (f) 180
(g) 420 (h) 240 (i) 360
(j) 28 (k) 40 (l) 63
(m) 450 (n) 54 (o) 5.6

Now try this!
The reason why the doubling and halving method works can be expressed in the following ways:
$a \times b = ab$
$\frac{1}{2} a \times 2b = \frac{1}{2} \times 2 \times ab = ab$

p 32
A1 (a) 87.6 cm^2 (b) 22 cm
(c) £68.40 (d) £10.75
(e) €43.20 (f) 45p
(g) 86.8 cm (h) £8
B1 (a) 31.5
(b) 22.4
(c) 49
(d) 2.2
(e) 2.3

p 33
C1 (a) 374 (b) 594 (c) 693
C2 (b) 418 517 649
(c) If the sum of the two digits is greater than 9, then the tens part of this number needs to be carried into the hundreds column.

Now try this!
Possible solutions:

$$12 \qquad 6$$
$$\times \qquad \times$$
$$1 \times 2 \times 3 \times 4$$
$$\times \qquad \times$$
$$24 \qquad 8$$

p 34
A (a) 13 (b) 7
39 21
5.2 3.5
2.6 0.7
(c) 36 (d) 66
4.8 2.2
2.4 11
7.2 68.2

p 35
C1 (a) 0.4 40% (b) 0.6 60%
(c) 0.8 80% (d) 0.75 75%
(e) 0.125 12.5% (f) 0.375 37.5%
C2 (a) 12 (b) 10
C3 (a) 11 g (b) 7.5 g (c) 6 g
(d) 14.25 g (e) 1.5 g (f) 8.8 g
C4 (a) $1\% = \frac{1}{100} = 0.1$
(b) $3\% = \frac{3}{100} = 0.3$
(c) $7\% = \frac{7}{100} = 0.7$
(d) $19\% = \frac{19}{100} = 0.19$
(e) $23\% = \frac{23}{100} = 0.23$
(f) $79\% = \frac{79}{100} = 0.79$

Now try this!

$\frac{1}{4}$	0.125	$\frac{1}{8}$	$\frac{3}{4}$
0.25	$\frac{1}{2}$	0.75	$1\frac{1}{2}$
$\frac{3}{4}$	$\frac{5}{8}$	$\frac{1}{4}$	$1\frac{5}{8}$
$1\frac{1}{2}$	$1\frac{1}{4}$	$1\frac{1}{8}$	

Total $3\frac{7}{8}$

p 36

A1 (a) 7×3
  18.75
(b) 8×4
  29.75
(c) 40×30
  1125
(d) 40×60
  2275
(e) 5×5
  24.75
(f) 8×20
  127.5
(g) 12×4
  43.75
(h) 14×6
  79.75
(i) 70×50
  3375
(j) 17×3
  43.75
(k) 8×11
  86.25

B (a) 16×5, 74.25
(b) 10×4, 35.7
(c) 15×12, 180.56
(d) 30×20, 569.6

p 37

C1 (a) $31 + 20$
(b) $410 - 230$
(c) 5×5
(d) $3500 + 6000$
(e) 50×5
(f) $50 \div 12$
(g) $8000 - 5000$
(h) $500 \div 20$
(i) $90 - 50$

Now try this!
(a) 1.4
(b) 16
(c) 1
(d) 1.2

p 38

A1 (a) $235 + 678 = 913$
(b) $534 + 183 = 717$
(c) $235 + 647 = 882$
(d) $677 + 678 = 1355$
(e) $848 + 275 = 1123$
(f) $5352 + 6974 = 12\,326$
(g) $889 - 678 = 211$
(h) $524 - 158 = 366$
(i) $1265 - 646 = 619$
(j) $635 - 519 - 116$
(k) $5945 - 1838 = 4107$
(l) $9052 - 6421 - 2628$

B1 (a) 546
(b) 87
(c) 12 749
(d) 1781

p 39

C1 (a) $5784 + 266 + 976$
(b) $4769 + 33\,681 + 976$
(c) $4769 + 266 + 5784$
(d) $45\,143 + 266 + 7649$
(e) $45\,143 + 33\,681 + 976$
(f) $45\,143 + 7649 + 33\,681$

C2 (a) $7649 - 5784$
(b) $5784 - 976$
(c) $33\,681 - 4769$

Now try this!
A = 4
B = 9
C = 5

p 40

A (a) 50.24
(b) 24.6
(c) 181.13
(d) 250.43
(e) 472.14
(f) 120.45

B (a) $33.6 + 51.7 = 85.3$
(b) $5.19 + 1.85 = 7.04$
(c) $2.44 + 6.78 = 9.22$
(d) $7.74 + 6.09 = 13.83$
(e) $3.5 + 2.75 = 6.25$
(f) $3.56 + 69.70 = 73.26$
(g) $8.89 - 6.73 = 2.16$
(h) $5.06 - 1.53 = 3.53$
(i) $15.68 - 6.4 = 9.28$
(j) $7.84 - 5.69 = 2.15$
(k) $59.45 - 18.30 = 41.15$
(l) $90.7 - 64.45 = 26.25$

p 41

C1 (c) 135.58 cannot be made.
C2 (a) $58.7 - 8.56 = 50.14$
(b) $134.6 - 64.59 = 70.01$
(c) $64.59 - 0.79 = 63.8$

Now try this!

24.15	**23.95**	24.95
43.3	24.35	5.4
5.6	24.75	42.7

p 42

A1 (a) 7475
(b) 5040
(c) 25 872
(d) 9178
A2 (a) 8316
(b) 22 737
(c) 18 095
B (a) 9234
(b) 8514
(c) 7154
(d) 10 584
(e) 30 044

p 43

C1 3288
3156
11 508
20 448
13 648
9408
21 132
36 848

Now try this!
132×45

p 44

A (a) 2
(b) 0.16
(c) 1.8
(d) 2.8
(e) 0.24
(f) 0.27
(g) 0.24
(h) 6.3
(i) 8.1
(j) 4.2
(k) 0.35
(l) 0.56
B1 (a) 25.4
(b) 20.88
(c) 59.85
(d) 28.72
B2 (a) 21.8
(b) 60.72
(c) 33.48
(d) 84.42

p 45

C1 (a) £26.46
(b) £25.88
(c) 10.08 m
(d) 22.95 kg
(e) £115.12
(f) 27.44 m
(g) £152.16
(h) 78.84 kg
(i) 83.04
(j) 144.72
C2 EQUIVALENT

Now try this!
(a) 1.23×4
(b) 4.31×2
(c) 32.1×4
(d) 14.2×3

p 46

A1 (a) 17
(b) 13
(c) 23
(d) 28
(e) 38
(f) 26
B (a) Answer wrong – should be 41.
(b) Remainder too large – answer should be 18.
(c) Subtraction error in line 3. Answer should be 24.

p 47

C (a) 782 ÷ 34   (b) 408 ÷ 68   (c) 986 ÷ 34
   (d) 578 ÷ 68   (e) 578 ÷ 85   (f) 986 ÷ 85

Now try this!
(a) £42   (b) £43   (c) £42.20
Question (c) has an answer closest to £42.50.

p 48

A1 (a) 12.4   (b) 8.4   (c) 9.8
    (d) 4.28   (e) 13.35   (f) 6.54

B

27.52	21.24	52.64
58.92	33.8	8.68
14.96	46.36	40.08

All rows, columns and diagonals add up to 101.4.

p 49

C1 (a) £23.96   (b) £9.79   (c) £15.32   (d) 36.2 m
    (e) £8.89   (f) 13.54 km (g) 12.36 m (h) 15.87

Now try this!
(a) 29.72   (b) 29.64   (c) £29.64
Question (a) is the odd one out

p 50

A1 (a) 127   (b) ⁻104   (c) ⁻306
    (d) ⁻182   (e) ⁻389   (f) ⁻308
    (g) ⁻311   (h) ⁻495   (i) 34
    (j) ⁻223   (k) ⁻91   (l) ⁻257
    (m) ⁻59   (n) ⁻4   (o) 19
    (p) ⁻34   (q) ⁻61   (r) ⁻1
    (s) 242   (t) 200   (u) 500
A2 (a) 225   (b) 361   (c) 729
    (d) 2116   (e) 5929   (f) 9801
    (g) 23   (h) 31   (i) 54
    (j) 65   (k) 73   (l) 98
B   (a) ⁻34   (b) ⁻52   (c) ⁻23
    (d) ⁻41   (e) ⁻323   (f) ⁻120

p 51

C1 All answers are given to 2 d.p.
    (a) ⁻5.31   (b) 0.37   (c) 0.14
    (d) ⁻6.25   (e) 3.55   (f) 7.39
    (g) 5.71   (h) 1.75   (i) 4.93
    (j) 0.98   (k) 0.32   (l) 77.44

Now try this!
(a) 1444   (b) 1444
(c) 3249   (d) 3249
Positive and negative squares give the same answer.

p 52

A1 (a) £233.60 (b) £97.20
    (c) £3.40   (d) 9p
    (e) 16p   (f) £24.30
    (g) £8.26   (h) 75p
    (i) 40p   (j) £3.67
    (k) £1.11   (l) £1.17
A2 (a) 1 hr 30 min
    (b) 1 hr 15 min
    (c) 1 hr 45 min   (d) 3 hr 45 min
    (e) 3 hr 15 min   (f) 1 hr 30 min
    (g) 13 hr 30 min   (h) 8 hr 45 min
B   (a) 1825   (b) 1020
    (c) 168   (d) 960
    (e) 2880   (f) 10 800

p 53

C1 (b) 36
    (c) £9
C2 (a) £9
    (b) £8
    (c) £13

Now try this!
(a) 19 days and 19 hours
(b) 39 days and 14 hours

p 54

B   (a) 101
    (b) 10 101
    (c) ⁻1

p 55

Now try this!
£5.55

p 56

B   (a) 5   (b) 6   (c) 2
    (d) 8   (e) 6   (f) 2
    (g) 8   (h) 5   (i) 4
    (j) 0   (k) 7   (l) 0
    (m) 9   (n) 9   (o) 2

p 57

C1 (a) ×   (b) ✓
    (c) ✓   (d) ×
    (e) ✓   (f) ×
    (g) ✓   (h) ×
    (i) ✓   (j) ×
    (k) ×   (l) ✓
    (m) ×   (n) ✓
    (o) ×   (p) ✓
    (q) ×   (r) ×

Now try this!
Approximate answers:
(a) 180   (b) 40
(c) 100   (d) 10
(e) 120   (f) 400

p 58

A   (a) 6 ÷ 75 should be 75 ÷ 6
    (b) £384 should be 384p or £3.84
    (c) 3.57 + 65 should be 3.57 + 0.65
    (d) 26 ÷ 5 should be 500 ÷ 26
B   (a) 12.5   (b) £3.84
    (c) £4.22   (d) 19

p 59

Now try this!
(a) 13
(b) 13
(c) 16